W9-BNP-438

What readers are saying:

The best book ever written about saving for college! This book unlocks the secrets of saving for college like the 401k plan did for saving for retirement. A real must for all families to understand.

A fantastic summary of 529 plans. This book should be read by anyone planning to send a child to college.

Terrific guide to a new way to save for college. Highly recommended. It's well-written, comprehensive, and objective, and it gave me enough information to make an informed decision.

Savingforcollege.com's

COMPLETE GUIDE
TO 529 PLANS

Savingforcollege.com's

COMPLETE GUIDE
TO 529 PLANS

2018/2019
12th Edition

Joseph F. Hurley, CPA
Kathryn Flynn
Matthew Toner, J.D.

Saving for College, LLC
Miami, FL

Savingforcollege.com's Complete Guide to 529 Plans

Published by:
Saving for College, LLC.
444 Brickell Ave.
Suite 820
Miami, FL 33131
INTERNET: www.savingforcollege.com
E-MAIL: support@savingforcollege.com

All rights are reserved. This book or any part of it may not be duplicated in any form or by any means, either electronically or mechanically without the written permission of the author. Short quotations may be included in book reviews, press releases, or magazine articles only if the author is credited.
Copyright © 2018 by Saving for College, LLC.

Disclaimer

The information contained in this book and related materials ("Information") is based on information from sources believed to be accurate and reliable and every reasonable effort has been made to make the book and related materials as complete and accurate as possible but such completeness and accuracy cannot be and is not guaranteed. The reader and user of the Information should use this book and related materials as a general guide and not as the ultimate source of information. This book and related materials are not intended to include every possible bit of information regarding the Information but rather to complement and supplement information otherwise available and the reader and user should use the Information accordingly. The Information contains information about tax and other laws and these laws may change. The reader and user should realize that any investment involves risk and the assumptions and projections used in the Information may not be how the investments turn out. The reader and user should consult with their own tax, financial and legal advisors about all of the Information.

THE INFORMATION IS PROVIDED ON AN "AS IS" BASIS WITHOUT ANY WARRANTIES OF ANY KIND, EXPRESS OR IMPLIED. THE AUTHORS, THE PUBLISHER, SAVING FOR COLLEGE, LLC, THE DISTRIBUTOR AND ANY OTHER PARTY EXPRESSLY DISCLAIM ANY LIABILITY FOR ANY LOSS OR DAMAGE INCLUDING BUT NOT LIMITED TO ANY LOSS OR DAMAGE FROM ANY USE OF ANY PART OF THE INFORMATION.

IF YOU DO NOT AGREE WITH ANY OF THE TERMS OF THE FOREGOING, YOU SHOULD *NOT* READ THIS BOOK. IF YOU DO NOT RETURN THIS BOOK, YOU WILL BE DEEMED TO HAVE ACCEPTED THE PROVISIONS OF THIS DISCLAIMER.

Table of Contents

Section One

529 Plans Explained

Section Two

State by State Comparisons

Available online at Savingforcollege.com/bestwaytosave

About Saving for College, LLC

Savingforcollege.com has been a leading independent authority on 529 college savings plans since 1999.

The site compiles and analyzes data, and creates content and tools to provide parents, financial professionals and state agencies with resources to help them understand how to meet the challenge of increasing education costs. Savingforcollege.com is regularly cited as an expert source on college savings information by prominent media publications. With over three million visitors each year, Savingforcollege.com serves the largest audience of college savers anywhere.

About the Authors

Joseph Hurley, C.P.A.

Joe Hurley launched Savingforcollege.com in 1999 while working as a tax CPA in Rochester, New York. He wrote and self-published the book *The Best Way to Save for College--A Complete Guide to 529 Plans* which has sold over 100,000 copies. Through the years Joe and his wife Ginny opened accounts with 529 plans in 34 states for their two children, both of whom are now graduated from college. (The reason for so many different accounts was to facilitate research of 529 plans.) Joe continues to write and speak about 529 plans and other college-savings topics while at the same time establishing Kettle Ridge Farm (maple syrup, honey, and shiitake mushrooms) and attending community college part-time with leftover 529 funds.

Kathryn Flynn

Kathryn is Content Director at Savingforcollege.com. She has been quoted in financial publications including the *Wall Street Journal,* the *New York Times, Fortune, Money* and *GOBankingRates,* and has been an expert guest on personal finance podcasts. Prior to Savingforcollege.com, Kathryn worked in product marketing at Henderson Global Investors (now Janus Henderson Investors), a global asset manager. She earned her MBA with Finance Concentration from DePaul University's Kellstadt Graduate

School of Business, and has prior FINRA Series 7 and 63 licenses. Kathryn has 529 college savings plans for each of her three children, and enjoys creating content to help other families prepare for future higher education costs.

Matthew Toner, J.D.

Matthew Toner is the director of institutional research at Savingforcollege.com and an expert on 529 plans. After obtaining his B.S. degree from the University of Florida and his J.D. from Florida State University, where he specialized in business law, Matthew went on to work as a financial advisor at Waddell & Reed. He holds his Series 7 and 66 licenses.

Visit www.savingforcollege.com

Here's Why

Our web site at www.savingforcollege.com is the perfect companion to this book. Here is what you will find when you visit:

- Section 2 of this book which includes state by state comparisons as well as exclusive access to innovative tools and calculators.
- Up-to-date descriptions of all 529 plans with links to their official websites.
- A 529 plan comparison tool, college savings calculator, and other useful tools.
- Federal, industry, and state news affecting 529 plans.
- Our exclusive "5-Cap Ratings" of all 529 plans.
- An active message board for those with questions, and for those with answers.
- Subscriber-only section containing quarterly investment performance rankings for all 529 savings plans, a portfolio expense look-up tool, underlying fund allocations, state tax calculators, and other resources for investment professionals.

Get exclusive online access to state by state comparisons and innovative tools and calculators.

Please visit www.savingforcollege.com/bestwaytosave

Introduction

Religion, morality, and knowledge, being necessary to good government and the happiness of mankind, schools and the means of education shall forever be encouraged.
NORTHWEST ORDINANCE, enacted by Congress July 13, 1787

For many young people in our society, a college degree is the key that unlocks the door to opportunity. The evidence comes from studies showing a wide disparity between the incomes of those who graduate from college and those who do not,[1] from the actions of our elected officials as they place college accessibility high on the nation's political agenda, and even from our own college experiences; many of us have seen our lives enriched and improved by the formal recognition of our academic achievements.

But college is expensive, and will become even more so in the future. This means that parents face a formidable challenge in paying for the higher education expenses of their children. Although a considerable amount of assistance is available to ease this burden, in the form of government support, student-aid programs, private scholarships, and perhaps some help from grandparents or other relatives, most parents cannot eliminate the need to prepare for the cost of sending their children to college. It becomes a matter of saving.

---

1. In 2010, the median annual earnings of full-time workers, ages 25–34, with at least a bachelor's degree was 50% higher than of those with only a high school diploma or equivalent. U.S. Department of Education, National Center for Education Statistics. (2012). *The Condition of Education 2012*, NCES 2012–045, Washington, DC: U.S. Government Printing Office.

This book is all about a remarkable savings program available to American families facing educational costs. Its formal name is the qualified tuition program, sometimes abbreviated as QTP, but more often referred to as a "Section 529 plan" or just plain "529 plan." Originally developed by the states, and given special status under federal tax law, it is a savings program you should know about. If you are looking for an effective way to save for your children, your grandchildren, or even yourself, a 529 plan may be a large part of the solution.

Section 529 refers to the specific provision in the Internal Revenue Code, our federal tax law, which describes this particular type of education savings vehicle and lays down some rules that the programs must abide by in order to assure their participants of its tax-beneficial treatment. Forty-nine states, and the District of Columbia, now operate a 529 plan. Some states have more than one. Many of these programs are open to residents of any state, and most of them offer the same benefits no matter if your child attends school in-state or out. In addition, the Private College 529 Plan was launched in 2003 as the first—and so far, the only—institutional prepaid tuition plan eligible for Section 529 treatment under an expansion of the law authorized by Congress in 2001. The Private College 529 Plan offers a prepayment program, without state involvement, on behalf of nearly 300 participating private colleges across the country.

The plethora of 529 plans creates a great deal of choice in your selection of a college savings program, and perhaps more than a little confusion. In addition, you will want to compare competing college-savings vehicles—including Coverdell education savings accounts, U.S. savings bonds, and mutual funds. By reading this book, you will be better prepared to make the right decisions for yourself and for your family.

How much does college cost?

According to the College Board, the price of one year at the average four-year private college for 2017–18, including published tuition and fees, room and board, and other expenses exceeded $46,000, and for the resident student at the average four-year public college or university the price was nearly $21,000.[2] During the past ten years, the annual rate of increase has averaged over five percent.

This trend is not new. Since 1980, college prices have been rising at a rate of two to three times the increase in the Consumer Price Index. If the pattern continues, the future sticker price of a four-year private-college degree for today's newborn will be in excess of $500,000, and for the student at a four-year public institution more than $225,000. Even more troubling is the fact that median family income has not been keeping pace with rising college costs.

Various policy groups and Congressional committees have become increasingly vocal in calling for colleges to control costs and make higher education more affordable for families. A provision contained in 2008 legislation to reauthorize the Higher Education Act (HEA) creates a tuition "watch list" identifying colleges with the largest percentage increases in tuition. The HEA also now requires that every postsecondary institution that participates in Title IV federal student aid programs provide an online "net price calculator" that estimates the net price of attendance (cost of attendance less grants and scholarships) for students and prospective students based on their individual circumstances.

Several wealthy universities, including Harvard and Stanford, have implemented changes in their financial-aid packages for families with incomes below certain levels. For example, the student with family income between $65,000 and $150,000 who attends Harvard will pay an amount not exceeding 10 percent of family income.

However, most Americans should not expect to see significant relief from the tuition spiral anytime soon. Several factors—including increasing costs relating to technology needs, campus improvements, and faculty salaries—suggest that college cost increases may continue to outpace the general inflation indices at least for the next several years.

For those who lack sufficient financial resources to simply pay the college bills when they arrive, the traditional means of outside assistance—federal, state, and institution-based financial-aid programs—will

---

2. The College Board, *Trends in College Pricing 2017* (Washington, D.C., 2017). The College Board is a nonprofit association serving students, schools and colleges. These figures are for students who are living away from home while attending college.

still be available. Indeed, the money available for student aid has picked up considerably in recent years after a long decline through the 1980s and early 1990s. During the ten years between 2007 and 2017, the federal government's investment in student aid through grants, loans and work-study doubled in current dollars, to $154 billion.[3] However, statistical averages fail to reflect the widening income disparity between high and low earners, and the growing problem of "unmet need" among lower-income students.

> To see how much college will cost when a beneficiary will be attending college, check out the College Cost Calculator at Savingforcollege.com/ccc.

How are families coping with these costs?

There is no shortage of surveys showing how families view and respond to the challenges of saving and paying for college. The bottom line is that many Americans do not feel adequately prepared.

- More than eight in 10 parents say they are willing to stretch themselves financially to obtain the best opportunity for their child (Sallie Mae and Ipsos, 2018).
- Eight in 10 parents cite concern about their child taking on significant debt as a factor motivating them to save more, and 85 percent of parents expect their child to graduate with debt, estimating an average $45,000 in student loans (Fidelity, 2017).
- In 2017, 60% of parents hoped to cover at least 75% of their child's college costs, yet only 40% were confident they would be able to pay for their child's referred university (Savingforcollege.com).

---

3. The College Board, *Trends in Student Aid 2017* (Washington, D.C. 2017).

Where is higher education on the nation's list of priorities?

Clearly, higher education is regarded in the halls of Congress and state capitols as a priority worthy of public subsidy. The nature of the subsidy has shifted, however, away from direct support of institutions in favor of tax incentives for individuals. Tax breaks now help the individual who is paying for college, and the one who is saving for college. More money is being invested in tax-advantaged college savings plans than ever before. In fact, over thirteen million 529-plan accounts are now being managed, and total assets in all 529 plans stood at over $317 billion at the end of 2017. With significant sums building up in their college-savings accounts, many families will be looking for the best college education that money can buy.

The turnaround in education-friendly tax legislation since the mid–1990s has been remarkable. Before 1996, only a few tax breaks were aimed at helping individuals pay for their own or their children's college expenses. They included the exclusion of interest on the redemption of certain U.S savings bonds used to pay for college costs; the employer-provided educational assistance plan, whereby an employee could receive up to $5,250 to pay for undergraduate costs as a tax-free benefit; and income exclusions for certain qualified scholarships received by an individual and, in narrow circumstances, for student loan forgiveness.

IRS Publication 970, Tax Benefits for Education, now describes 11 separate tax incentives targeted to families paying for postsecondary education. In a span of just two years—1996 and 1997—Congress approved 529 plans, the Education IRA (now the Coverdell education savings account), two separate but related tuition credits (the Hope credit and the Lifetime Learning credit), and a waiver of the 10 percent penalty on premature distributions from an IRA to pay college expenses. In 2001, employer-provided educational assistance plans were expanded to include graduate school costs, and new tax deductions were approved for the payment of college tuition and for the payment of interest on college-related debts. And then in 2009, the American Opportunity tax credit was created, replacing the Hope credit and providing an even richer incentive for college attendance.

Traditional means of saving for college

Families who could afford to set aside savings for education purposes before the advent of tax-advantaged 529 plans and Coverdell education savings accounts still had several options. They could establish investment accounts for children and grandchildren, either in the parents' or grandparents' names; in the child's name in an UGMA or UTMA account; or in special education trusts drafted by attorneys and trust companies. Zero coupon municipal bonds, stock mutual funds, and insurance products offered some degree of tax relief and were often the investments of choice within these accounts.

But in the face of the new tax-advantaged savings vehicles, the traditional approaches to college saving have rapidly lost popularity. Although favorable tax rates on long-term capital gains and qualified dividends can effectively reduce the tax burden in traditional accounts, those rates jumped at the beginning of 2013 for high-income taxpayers and may rise further under any future "tax reform." Furthermore, the opportunity to shift investment income to a child's tax bracket is much more limited now that the "kiddie tax" applies to many children as old as 23 years (see chapter 11).

How confusing are all these incentives?

Unfortunately, they can be very confusing. There are now so many alternatives available that you are likely to have a difficult time selecting the ones that are most appropriate in your circumstances. And some of these options are mutually exclusive; your use of one program may restrict or eliminate the use of another. During Congressional hearings held in July 2012, the U.S. Government Accountability Office testified that 14 percent of eligible filers in 2009, representing over 1.5 million tax returns, failed to maximize the federal tax benefits available for payment of postsecondary education costs. The good news is that Congress now recognizes the unprecedented level of complexity in the maze of education tax benefits and before long is likely to consolidate and simplify those benefits.[4]

---

4. Hearings before the U.S. Senate Committee on Finance (July 25, 2012).

Why focus on 529 plans?

Section 529 plans provide some powerful and unique tax advantages not available with other education-savings options. What other tax-advantaged program allows everyone to participate, without regard to age or income level? What other program allows the accumulation of over $300,000 in a tax-sheltered account for one child's education expenses? What other mechanism allows someone with a large estate to immediately reduce that estate by $75,000 per child (or grandchild) without triggering gift tax, and without giving up control of the assets?

The answer is that no other tax-advantaged program provides the combination of benefits 529 plans offer. They are unique and powerful creations that come in as many different variations as there are states and institutions to sponsor them. They are intended to serve one purpose—providing a way for families of any income level to save for future educational costs in the most effective way possible. But they also have investment, tax, retirement, and estate-planning implications that reach far beyond this one purpose.

This book will help you make the most effective use of the savings opportunities presented by 529 plans. It explains the many strategies to consider and choices to make before deciding to enroll in a 529 plan, and, once enrolled, the changes you can make along the way. This book also compares 529 plans to the other alternatives available to a family in saving for college, so that the best options can be selected from the array of choices.

Glossary

A number of terms used in this book deserve some explanation. An effort has been made to use the most common terminology, although not necessarily the language found in tax law, and to be as consistent as possible in the use of the terms. You will find, however, that the various state programs and other descriptive resources are not uniform in this regard.

529 plan—a qualified tuition program described in Section 529 of the Internal Revenue Code. This may also be referred to as a **Section 529 Plan** or **QTP**.

Account owner—the person with ownership and control of the 529 account, usually but not necessarily the **contributor to the account** or **purchaser of the contract**. Many 529 plans refer to the account owner as the **participant**.

Basis—the sum of all cash contributed or paid into the account, plus the basis portion of qualifying rollovers to the account, less the basis portion of distributions previously made from the account. The basis is also called the **principal of the account** or the **investment in the account**.

Designated beneficiary—the individual for whom the account or contract is established. All 529 plans require a designated beneficiary be named for each contract or account, except for accounts established by state or local governments or 501(c)(3) charitable organizations for scholarship purposes.

Distribution—an amount of cash withdrawn from a 529 account, or the value of educational benefits provided by a 529 plan. Most 529 savings programs use the term **withdrawal**. Distributions not in excess of the designated beneficiary's qualified higher education expenses are called **qualified distributions** or **qualified withdrawals**. Distributions in excess of the designated beneficiary's qualified higher education expenses are called **nonqualified distributions, nonqualified withdrawals,** or **refunds**.

Earnings—the total account value less the basis. Distributions from a 529 plan consist of pro-rated amounts of earnings and basis.

Prepaid program—a type of 529 plan (another type, the savings program, is described below) that promises to pay the beneficiary's future college tuition and other specified costs in return for your purchase of the program's prepaid educational arrangement or contract. Prepaid programs that sell tuition by the semester or year are referred to in this book as **contract-type prepaid programs**. Some prepaid programs offer units, with the value of each unit pegged to a fixed percentage (often 1%) of one year's tuition. These programs are referred to in this book as **unit-type prepaid programs**.

Private prepaid program—a 529 plan operated by an eligible educational institution, not by a state. The only existing private prepaid program is the Private College 529 Plan.

Qualified higher education expenses (QHEE) —the postsecondary education expenses incurred by a designated beneficiary that are counted in determining the tax treatment of distributions from a 529 plan. Section 529 describes the types of higher education expenses that qualify, generally tuition, fees, books, supplies, equipment, additional expenses of special needs beneficiaries, and a limited amount of room and board. The 2017 Tax Cuts and Jobs Act expanded the definition of QHEE to include up to $10,000 in private K-12 tuition expenses.

Rollover—a transfer of funds between 529 plans that is not treated as a distribution because it satisfies certain conditions under Section 529.

Savings program—a type of 529 plan (another type, the prepaid program, is described above) in which a **contribution to an account is invested in** a portfolio of mutual funds or other types of underlying investments. Most 529 savings programs offer a menu of portfolios, or **investment options,** from which to select. The value of the account is determined by the performance of the underlying investments. Some states will refer to their 529 savings program as an **investment program** to underscore the fact that accounts can lose value.

ONE

History of 529 Plans

The states—not the federal government—deserve the credit for inventing 529 plans. Section 529 was not even part of the Internal Revenue Code at the time Michigan Governor James J. Blanchard, in his January 1986 State-of-the-State Address, proposed the creation of a new state-run prepaid tuition program "designed to help parents guarantee to their children the opportunity of a Michigan college education." With tuition costs spiraling, such a program would address the increasing anxiety in many thousands of Michigan households. The result of this proposal was the Michigan Education Trust (MET), a newly-created fund to which the state's residents could pay a stipulated amount in exchange for the trust's promise to pay future tuition for a named beneficiary at any Michigan public college or university. The essential benefit was the opportunity to prepay future tuition so as not to be affected by future tuition increases.

The Michigan proposal generated interest in other states, with Wyoming and Florida the first to launch prepaid tuition programs of similar design. Michigan delayed its own launch so that a ruling could be requested from the Internal Revenue Service regarding the tax aspects of the arrangement. The IRS responded to Michigan with both good news and bad news.[1] The good news was that the purchaser of the "prepaid tuition contract" would not be taxed on the accruing value of the contract until the year in which funds were distributed or refunded. The bad news was that the trust established by the state of Michigan to receive prepayments and operate the program would be subject to income tax on earnings from the invested funds. According to the IRS, the trust did not qualify as a tax-exempt state instrumentality.

Lacking IRS' full blessing, MET went ahead anyway and in 1988 began entering into prepaid tuition contracts with Michigan's residents. Fifty-five thousand individuals signed up for the program. MET paid federal income tax on its investment earnings, and in 1990 filed suit for refund from the IRS. The case was first decided in favor of the IRS, but on appeal in 1994, the Sixth Circuit Court of Appeals reversed the district court judge's decision and found in Michigan's favor.[2]

The irony of the Michigan experience is that MET was forced in 1990 to stop issuing new contracts, due not so much to the burden of paying income taxes, but because it had been selling the prepaid tuition contracts at prices later determined to be too low. When originally establishing contract pricing, program administrators had relied on overly optimistic projections of the rate of return on invested funds in relation to the trust's obligation to pay for rising tuition prices. Simply put, the trust was headed towards insolvency. (The program later resumed with more appropriate pricing and remains today as one of the largest and most successful prepaid programs.)

Not long after its 1994 defeat in the Sixth Circuit, the IRS began considering other ways to keep participants in prepaid tuition programs from gaining a tax advantage, one of which was to tax beneficiaries each year on the increasing value of their prepayment contracts. Concerned that such treatment would be a disincentive for savings, Congress passed new legislation authorizing qualified State tuition programs ("QSTPs") as part of the Small Business Job Protection Act of 1996. Section 529 was added to the

---

1. IRS Letter Ruling 8825027

2. Michigan v. United States, 40 F.3rd 817 (6th Cir. 1994), rev'g 802 F. Supp. 120 (W.D. Mich 1992)

Internal Revenue Code by the Act, conferring tax exemption to qualifying state programs, and deferring tax on participants' undistributed earnings.

Although the enactment of Section 529 attracted little notice at the time, it no doubt helped to advance the Clinton administration's highly-publicized agenda to create significant new tax incentives for higher education, an effort that culminated a year later with the Taxpayer Relief Act of 1997 (TRA). The TRA introduced the Hope and Lifetime Learning credits, a tax deduction for interest on student loans, and penalty-free IRA withdrawals for higher education. Substantial changes were also made to Code Section 529 by the TRA, adding room and board to the list of qualifying expenses and providing special estate and gift tax treatment for participants in a 529 plan.

The TRA also gave rise to a new tax-advantaged savings vehicle for college named the Education IRA. Unlike Section 529, which provided that earnings were taxable even when withdrawn for qualified higher education expenses (albeit at the student's tax rate), the Education IRA offered federal tax exemption for the earnings when withdrawn for the same purpose. While this was seen as a significant advantage, the Education IRA was hobbled by age and income restrictions, and by a $500 annual per-beneficiary contribution limit.

With the ink barely dry on the 1997 TRA, the Republican-controlled Congress began pressing to make tax-free Education IRA distributions available to families sending their children to private and parochial grade schools. A bill was drafted to add elementary and secondary school expenses as approved expenses. With much less fanfare, another provision was added to the bill to make Section 529 distributions tax-free, not just tax-deferred, when used for college. Although the bill passed Congress, President Bill Clinton vetoed it, likening the expanded Education IRA to private school vouchers. A similar effort in 1999 failed for the same reason.

The stage was set for President George W. Bush when he took office in January 2001. New tax bills were crafted in both the Senate and the House of Representatives containing the previously-vetoed changes. With strong bipartisan support, the Economic Growth and Tax Relief Reconciliation Act (EGTRRA) of 2001 was signed into law on June 7, 2001. The expansion of the Education IRA exemption to include qualifying expenses for kindergarten through 12th grade, along with an increase in the annual contribution limit from $500 to $2,000, were hailed as major accomplishments. (Soon after EGTRRA's enactment, the Education IRA was renamed the Coverdell education savings account, giving recognition to Senator Paul Coverdell as champion of the K–12 provision.)

The favorable changes made by EGTRRA to Section 529 received relatively little notice at the time, but have turned out to have much more impact on families' college savings. Not only did qualified distributions from 529 plan gain tax-free status for federal purposes—and for state tax purposes in those states that piggyback on the federal tax treatment—but other major improvements came along as well. The requirement that states collect a penalty on nonqualified distributions was replaced by a 10 percent tax penalty to be paid with the federal tax return; same-beneficiary rollovers between 529 plans were now permissible, albeit restricted to one rollover per beneficiary in any 12-month period; and educational institutions were given permission to establish their own 529 prepaid tuition programs without any state involvement, thus requiring that the formal name for these programs change from qualified State tuition programs (QSTP) to qualified tuition programs (QTP).

Due to federal budget constraints, EGTRRA was made subject to a general sunset clause, such that every tax provision within the new law would expire on December 31, 2010. In effect, the improvements to Section 529, to the Education IRA, and to many other parts of the tax law were merely temporary. If any of the changes were to last beyond 2010, it would be up to Congress and the president to extend them through subsequent legislation.

With improved federal tax treatment, and in spite of the 2010 sunset, new 529 plans began springing up across the country, creating a wave of enthusiasm among the professional financial community and capturing the interest of the press. An institution-sponsored 529 plan representing over 200 private colleges, the Independent 529 Plan (later renamed Private College 529 Plan), was launched. Articles and feature stories extolling the benefits of 529 plans were appearing at an increasing pace in the national and regional media. And substantial dollars were finding their way into 529 plans: the $9 billion invested at the beginning of 2001 jumped to nearly $27 billion by the end of 2002.

In January 2003, the momentum was temporarily disrupted by the Bush administration's proposal to establish new Lifetime Savings Accounts (LSAs), which would permit individuals of any age and income level to contribute up to $7,500 annually to an investment account, and take withdrawals at any time and for any purpose free from federal income tax. The flexibility and simplicity of the LSA promised to attract a substantial number of college savers, along with their investment dollars. Failing to gain any traction in Congress, the LSA proposal withered, and assets in 529 plans grew by another $18 billion in 2003, to over $45 billion.

As the level of assets and number of accounts grew, so did the anxiety over the looming expiration of the 529 tax exclusion at the end of 2010. The media and many financial advisors became cautious when discussing or writing about 529 plans, and the pace of contributions began to slow. The Pension Protection Act of 2006 (PPA) ultimately saved the day for 529 plans and their millions of participants. In the final hours before its passage, Congressional leaders agreed to insert a provision in the PPA that would make permanent all of EGTRRA's changes to Section 529, including tax-free treatment for qualified distributions. President Bush signed the law in August 2006. With the cloud of uncertainty lifted, contributions once again began pouring in to 529 plans, and by the end of 2007, assets in all 529 plans totaled nearly $130 billion.

But as the economy and financial markets headed south in 2008, so did assets in 529 plans, finishing the year at only $105 billion. Concerns over "losses" in college savings accounts, and being "locked in" to undesired investment options, captured headlines in the financial press. The IRS reacted by issuing a notice to 529 plans (Notice 2009-01) that increased the number of permitted investment changes in a 529 account from one per year to two per year. The increased flexibility was temporary, however, and applied to 2009 only.

In December 2015, President Obama signed the Protecting Americans from Tax Hikes (PATH) Act, which made several important changes to 529 plans. Perhaps the most notable update was the permanent addition of computers and related technology, including internet access, to the list of qualified higher education expenses, mirroring a provision already enjoyed by Coverdell education savings accounts related to K-12 expenses.

The PATH Act also eliminated an administrative reporting requirement that many say has increased paperwork and thus the cost on plan administrators, and waived the 10% penalty tax on refunded 529 money if it is deposited back into a 529 account within 60 days. As the economy slowly gained strength after 2009, 529 plans began growing again and have continued to grow since. Assets in all 529 plans rose to $317.6 billion by December 31, 2017, a 15.4 percent increase from the $275.1 billion a year earlier. In addition, the total number of accounts increased from 12.8 million to 13.2 million over the same time period.[3]

Changes to the structure and marketing of 529 plans over the years have contributed to their growth. Often at the behest of the investment firms hired to operate their 529 plans, many states early on opened up marketing and distribution outside state borders to a national audience. Today we see a large number of these widely-available programs being distributed under selling agreements with broker-dealers. By partnering with the professional investment community, the states are able to offer 529 plans with the look and feel of mutual funds. Registered brokers and investment advisors can directly assist families in understanding 529 plans and selecting appropriate investments, whereas state program administrators are generally prohibited from providing investment advice.

Most recently, the 2017 Tax Cuts and Jobs Act has expanded 529 plan benefits to include tax-free withdrawals for private, public or religious elementary, middle and high school tuition. Effective January 1, 2018, families can now use 529 plans to pay for up to $10,000 in K-12 tuition expenses per beneficiary per year. It's important to remember that state tax breaks, such as deductions for contributions to 529 plans, or state tax-free 529 withdrawals, are only available when the funds are withdrawn to pay for expenses that the state considers qualified, which may or may not include K-12 tuition. States are currently reviewing the impact of the federal tax change to determine whether updates to state legislation are required.

At the state level, non-qualified withdrawals may be subject to state income tax and, in some cases, a penalty on the earnings portion. You may also have to repay any deductions or credits claimed.

---

3. College Savings Plans Network at www.collegesavings.org, 529 Plan Data report, December 31, 2017.

To see which states currently
consider K-12 tuition a qualified expense,
visit Savingforcollege.com/k-12

Investment offerings available through 529 savings programs have also evolved over the years. The earliest programs offered a single fixed-income investment. In the late 1990s, several states introduced an "age-based" investment strategy providing a blend of equity and fixed-income investments. The allocation would shift to a more conservative mix as the beneficiary approached college age. The age-based option was seen as particularly useful in light of Section 529's prohibition on investment direction, which prevented participants from changing investments on their own.

Next was the introduction of "static" or "fixed-allocation" investment options as alternatives to the age-based approach, creating a menu of investment offerings for the program participant. These options appealed to investors who desired more control over their asset allocation. Unfortunately, the prohibition on investment direction meant that a program participant in the early years could not later change his mind and opt for a different investment option within his 529 account.

Most investors were not truly locked in. A "rollover" made it possible to move funds to a different 529 account in the plan, or to another state's 529 plan, and end up with different investments. Originally, however, a rollover was tax-free only if the beneficiary designation was changed to a member of the original beneficiary's family. The 2001 EGTRRA made things significantly easier, permitting a same-beneficiary rollover between programs once in any 12-month period. The IRS, sensing the prohibition against participant investment direction contained in Section 529 had become a paper tiger in the wake of EGTRRA, subsequently announced in September 2001 (Notice 2001–55) that a program could permit investors to change their investment selection once every calendar year, or whenever a beneficiary change took place. No longer was it necessary to transfer 529 funds to another 529 plan in order to effect a change in investments.

Whereas in their early years 529 plans were largely viewed as somewhat quirky and of limited usefulness, by 2002 they had broken out into the mainstream. Their tax advantages, investment offerings and near-universal accessibility now made them attractive to the majority of families in a position to save for college. The states have ceded much of their direct involvement in running the programs to the large financial institutions that are more experienced and effective in marketing and managing an investment product. And they have allowed their programs to be marketed across state lines to a national audience, injecting a competitive element that occasionally tests the collegial atmosphere in which states' elected officials and agency heads have worked together to develop and promote the concept of 529 plans.

Why do the states decide to operate 529 plans?

Besides Wyoming, which dismantled its program in 2006, every state offers at least one 529 savings or prepaid tuition program. (Even before Congress fully sanctioned 529 plans in 1996, nine states had been operating prepaid tuition programs for their residents.) The states' commitment to 529 plans doesn't end with merely offering a program. Thirty-four of the 41 states with a personal income tax, along with the District of Columbia, offer their residents a state income tax deduction or credit for some or all of their contributions to the home-state 529 plan (and in six of these states, to an out-of-state plan as well). And many times we see states embellishing their 529 plans with matching contribution programs, laws protecting account assets from the claims of creditors, scholarship contests, and other incentives.

But why do the states make this commitment? Expenditures for staff and other state resources in establishing and maintaining a 529 plan can be significant and state tax subsidies can be costly. Few states expect to see any net revenue from program fees charged to participant accounts.

The primary reason for the states' interest in 529 plans is the conviction that education is an essential function of state government, and that establishing tax-advantaged savings programs targeted for education allows more individuals to obtain a college degree without taking on a crushing debt load. This argument is met with some degree of skepticism, however, since the amount of direct support provided by many states to their public systems of higher education has not kept pace with costs, forcing state schools to increase their tuition to even higher levels.

Some cynics also believe that the primary motivation for states to commit money in establishing and maintaining 529 plans is political. The programs allow elected officials to look good to the voters. Education is a powerful campaign issue. The governor and state treasurer who champion legislation making it easier for people to afford a college education will take credit for being "pro-family." Some of the impetus and support for the expanding 529 market comes from the National Association of State Treasurers, which has formed an affiliate, the College Savings Plans Network (CSPN), as a means to coordinate resources among its members and share ideas concerning state-sponsored programs. Composed of state officials and program administrators, CSPN meets at least annually to discuss issues and communicate ideas and new developments.

Most of the older 529 plans were developed by the states as prepaid programs, while the majority of newer 529 plans are savings programs (see chapter 5 for a comparison of the two program types). Many prepaid programs are restricted to state residents and cover only undergraduate tuition and fees. Savings programs are generally more flexible in their application to all the qualifying costs of higher education, and are more familiar to American families accustomed to IRAs and 401(k) plans. Savings programs are also easier to administer and less costly to the state, particularly when an outside financial-services company is willing to offer turnkey management under attractive financial arrangements with the state.

How are 529 plans regulated?

As a state-issued security, an interest in a 529 plan is not subject to the same level of federal oversight as most other types of securities and is exempt from registration with the Securities and Exchange Commission (SEC). However, the SEC can still bring suit against a state or its 529 administrative agency when alleging fraud.

The Municipal Securities Rulemaking Board (MSRB), a self-regulatory agency created by Congress and subject to SEC administrative oversight, has broad regulatory authority over the sale of 529 plans by "dealers" and has been active in issuing new investor-protection rules. The Financial Industry Regulatory Agency (FINRA) enforces the MSRB's rules, along with its own.

As the college-savings industry has grown, these federal regulators have increased their scrutiny of 529 plans and the sales practices surrounding them. Much of the attention has been focused on the sale of out-of-state 529 plans by brokers to residents of states offering tax deductions and other benefits for participation in the home-state 529 plan. In 2006, the MSRB finalized a set of disclosure requirements and suitability standards for brokers selling out-of-state 529 plans, which became effective in August of that year.[4] FINRA's enforcement efforts have been aimed at ensuring that its member broker-dealers install appropriate policy and supervisory procedures in connection with sale of 529 plans by registered representatives, and several member firms have faced fines for insufficient supervisory procedures and other infractions.

But because federal authority extends only to 529 plans distributed through dealers, several of the direct-sold 529 savings programs, along with prepaid tuition programs, have only their own states to answer to. The states are intent on preserving their right to self-regulate 529 plans, and depend in large part on the College Savings Plans Network (CSPN) to define and coordinate self-regulatory efforts. (In practice, the direct-sold 529 plans generally attempt to conform to the same standards required by the MSRB of dealer-distributed 529 plans.)

In 2004, public criticism of 529 plans increased after several programs were singled out for charging high expenses or providing insufficient disclosure to investors. Subcommittees of both the U.S. House of Representatives and the Senate held hearings to explore these issues and to question the ability of the states to self-regulate 529 plans. In response, CSPN accelerated its efforts on behalf of the states to formulate disclosure guidelines for 529 savings plans. The initial guidelines were approved in mid–2004 and adopted by nearly all states. The guidelines have since been revised several times and adopted by all the states, and they have proven to

---

4. MSRB Notice 2006–23 (August 7, 2006)

be very beneficial to investors.

Why have states been allowed to restrict their incentives to the in-state 529 plan?

The federal tax advantages with 529 plans are the same regardless of which particular 529 plan you decide to use. But states are free to offer extra incentives to college savers, and to restrict those incentives to their own 529 plans. For example, every state with a matching contribution program will invest the match dollars in its own 529 plan. Also, 28 out of the 35 states—if you include the District of Columbia—offering a tax deduction or credit for contributions deny the benefit for any contributions made to an out-of-state 529 plan.

But seven states have adopted "tax parity." They offer their taxpayers the same state tax benefit for investing in an out-of-state 529 plan that they earn for investing in the home-state 529 plan. The tax-parity states, in order of legislative approval, are Kansas, Pennsylvania, Arizona, Arkansas, Missouri, Montana, and Minnesota. Parity legislation has been and will continue to be considered in several other states. For several reasons, however, many state legislatures, treasurers, and governors oppose the notion of tax parity. They may wish to retain a competitive advantage for the home state 529 plan; they may oppose the notion of using state tax dollars to subsidize other states' 529 plans over which have no control; or they simply find tax parity to be too costly when approving state budgets.

A case that came before the Supreme Court in 2007 threatened the states' right to restrict their 529 benefits to the states' own 529 plans. In *Kentucky Department of Revenue v. Davis*, the plaintiffs challenged the right of Kentucky to exempt interest income on Kentucky bonds while imposing Kentucky tax on interest from out-of-state municipal bonds, arguing that such tax discrimination was unconstitutional. The Supreme Court ultimately ruled in Kentucky's favor.[5] Had the Davises prevailed, there would have followed a rash of similar lawsuits against any state that restricts its tax benefits to the in-state 529 plan.

---

5. *Department of Revenue of Kentucky et al. v. Davis et ux,* 553 U.S. ___ (2008)

What's in store for the future?

The future for 529 plans is exceptionally bright. Favorable federal legislation in the areas of tax, financial aid, and asset protection; ongoing program improvements and lowering of expenses; generous state incentives; positive media coverage; and the ever-increasing cost of sending a child to college all point to the increasing popularity of 529 plans and a surge of new contributions.

We have seen a push for additional expansion of 529 plans in recent years, with over a dozen proposals submitted by the House and Senate. Significant proposed changes include (1) Excluding employer contributions to 529 plans from the employee's gross income, (2) increasing the contribution limit Coverdell education savings accounts, (3) creating a non-refundable tax credit of up to $2,000 for 529 plan contributions made by low-income taxpayers, (4) allowing 529 plan balances to be rolled over into a Roth IRA after 10 years, and (5) excluding 529 plans and prepaid tuition plans from the definition of assets on the Free Application for Federal Student Aid (FAFSA).

Perhaps the biggest challenge to the continuing growth of 529 plans comes from competing tax-advantaged vehicles—particularly IRAs and defined-contribution retirement plans—that can soak up a family's available savings. Now that 529 plans can be used to pay for K-12 tuition, the Coverdell education savings account no longer poses much of a threat. However, families can still use a Coverdell education savings account to pay for qualified elementary and secondary expenses not covered by a 529 plan.

A future president and the U.S. Treasury Department may even resurrect proposals for the Lifetime Savings Account. But even if the LSA were to make it through Congress, the chances of its being watered down in the process are high. And while any new federal tax-advantaged savings vehicle could significantly impair the growth of 529 plans, the impact would not be fatal. Section 529 plans will continue under any circumstances to offer several key benefits—e.g. state tax breaks, tuition prepayment options, and high contribution limits—that LSAs could never match.

And these key benefits seem here to stay. In January 2015, President Obama released a proposal to dismantle the federal tax incentive of 529 plans. The administration framed the proposal as leveling the educational playing field by abolishing a tax break for the wealthy and redirecting the funds to middle class families. But rebuttals were quickly delivered, calling it an attack on ordinary Americans looking to save for their children's future. Members of Congress on both sides of the aisle joined in, as did angry parents from across the country.

The public outcry was so saturated that the administration dropped the proposal a handful of days later. It seemed the administration misjudged the important role these tax-advantaged account play in people's lives. The political miscalculation goes to show that 529 plans are officially a part of the American Dream. And as the popularity of these accounts grow, the chance someone proposes to harm them diminishes.

We will continue to witness the evolution of the 529 plans. Many states will continue to press for further improvements in their programs, although some may ultimately decide that they can no longer compete in the college-savings marketplace on their own and will seek to join forces with other states by combining plans, or will shutter their plans and refer participants to other states' plans, as Wyoming and Tennessee have done in the past. Several of the larger investment firms, and perhaps a few smaller ones as well, will be committing substantial resources to gain or maintain a foothold in the burgeoning 529 industry, while others that are currently involved may decide to drop out. (Wells Fargo—the former program manager for Wisconsin's 529 plans—decided to exit the 529 management business in 2012).

TWO

Why You Should Consider a 529 Plan

As everyone knows, children "grow up too fast." Yet, too few parents make a serious attempt to figure out how much it will cost to send their children to college, or consider available options in planning for those costs. Perhaps you expect your child to receive a full athletic or other merit scholarship to a major university. Is your seventh-grader already up to six-foot-four and able to hit four out of five from beyond the three-point line? Was she the national champ in her age group for the 200-meter butterfly? Has he been the headline performer at Carnegie Hall? If so, congratulations! College costs should not be a problem for you, assuming your child's injury-free dedication to the sport or other activity continues through high school. If not, welcome to the group of us who cannot count on a full scholarship and need to face the prospect of coming up with the resources to fund our child's education.

That prospect can be overwhelming. Let's face it, just meeting everyday expenses is challenging enough, never mind trying to save significant dollars on top of that. It is difficult to conceptualize the amount that the experts are telling us a private college will cost in 2036 when today's newborn will be enrolling. Over $500,000? Why even bother to try?

Some of us believe there will always be other ways to pay for college if personal savings are not sufficient. Thanks to our educational institutions and government, a safety net currently does exist, in the form of federal, state, and institution-based financial-aid programs. But even with the programs now available—including loans, grants, and work-study—many qualified students and their families face financial pressures that impact their desire and ability to attend college.

And then there's the question of priorities: college savings versus retirement savings. The common advice is to satisfy your retirement needs before attempting to save for college. After all, no bank will offer you a loan for your retirement. But generalized advice is not always the best advice. Certainly, you will want to take advantage of a match offered by your employer into your 401(k) plan. But beyond that, no one should fault you for your decision to build a college savings account with money that might otherwise be saved for retirement. In fact, a 2016 survey by T. Rowe Price found that 76% of parents said they would delay their retirement to pay for their kids' college education.

Before 529 plans came along, some parents were unwilling to establish dedicated college savings accounts even when they had the resources to do so. Putting assets in a Uniform Gifts to Minors Act (UGMA) or Uniform Transfers to Minors Act (UTMA) account was often recommended as a way to shelter college savings from income taxes, but many parents were reluctant to accept the risk that the child will decide to fund an "alternative" lifestyle that does not include college. Alternatively, they could place the assets in trust with provisions that prevent unauthorized use of the funds, but the establishment of the trust may involve significant time and money, and then it requires annual maintenance. This left home equity, bank savings accounts, and taxable mutual funds as the primary vehicles for college savings.

But now, 529 plans offer an attractive alternative, with their many features and tax incentives to overcome families' reluctance to save for college. In fact, they are likely to be your best option for college savings if you have school-age children or grandchildren and are looking to invest significant amounts of money (tens or even hundreds of thousands of dollars).

If your savings goals are more modest, the 529 plan remains competitive with Coverdell education savings accounts (chapter 9) and other college savings strategies designed for investors with more limited resources. No matter what your family's circumstances—large or small, low-income or high-income, decided on a particular college or undecided, transient or settled—there are 529 plans available to accommodate your college saving desires in simple, flexible, and tax-efficient ways. In fact, 529 plans offer advantages even to those without school-age children or grandchildren. Who's to say that the older individual will not want to return to school at some point in the future? We see more "nontraditional" students enrolling in postsecondary schools every year, for graduate work, for a change of career, or just for enjoyment and self-improvement. A 529 plan can be a great way to save for this possibility, even if the idea is eventually abandoned.

What's so great about 529 plans?

Here are the advantages, in a nutshell:

Federal income tax advantages

- ◆ Earnings build up in your account on a tax-deferred basis.
- ◆ Distributions from your account that are used for qualifying education expenses are tax-free.

Estate and gift tax benefits

- ◆ Your contributions to a 529 account are treated as completed, present-interest gifts to the beneficiary for purposes of the federal gift tax and generation-skipping transfer tax. The money comes out of your taxable estate, and the gifts qualify for the $15,000 gift-tax annual exclusion.
- ◆ A special election allows your contributions to be treated as if they were made over a five-year period for gift and generation-skipping

transfer tax purposes. This means that $75,000 can be contributed to a 529 plan account gift-tax free (assuming you make no other gifts during that five-year period).

Availability and flexibility

- Unlike so many other tax breaks, a 529 plan imposes no income limitations. A high-income individual can take advantage of a 529 plan when other alternatives (such as a Coverdell education savings account) are not available.
- In most 529 plans, over $400,000 can be contributed to an account for a single beneficiary. At $2,000 per year, a Coverdell education savings account just doesn't measure up.
- Despite the treatment of your contributions as completed gifts, you still retain ownership and control of the account. This creates powerful and unique advantages. You, not the beneficiary, decide when to take distributions and for what purpose. You can change the beneficiary of the account; you can even revoke the assets. Any concern that you may have about losing control of your investments is greatly diminished.

Investment benefits

- 529 plans offer a variety of options, providing the opportunity to select an approach that matches your own investment objectives. Some programs offer a way for your savings to keep up with increases in tuition costs; others offer a menu of investments from which to select, ranging from low-risk, fixed-income funds to higher-risk stock funds; while still others will automatically allocate your account among stocks, bonds and money market investments based on the age of your beneficiary or the number of years to expected matriculation. Many programs have no residency requirements, making the range of savings options available to all.
- You can obtain professional investment management at a reasonable cost. Fees and expenses will vary considerably among 529 plans, and

they should always be a factor in your decision to invest. But for most families the tax benefits of a 529 plan outweigh the extra expense, and the sponsoring states are intent on keeping the costs as low as possible, particularly for their own residents. Some programs utilizing mutual funds are able to acquire the lowest-cost "institutional" shares, thereby reducing the overall expense to you.

♦ Many programs accommodate automatic payment plans through payroll deduction or electronic funds transfer from your bank account, making education budgeting simple and providing the discipline that some parents need.

State tax benefits

♦ Nearly all states follow federal income tax treatment in excluding the earnings in your 529 account from state and local income taxes when used to pay for qualified education expenses, and many offer a deduction or tax credit for all or part of your contributions into their programs.

♦ A few states also provide other financial benefits to program participants, such as scholarships, matching contributions, or favorable treatment in determining eligibility for state-funded financial aid.

Asset protection

♦ In some states, the law provides specific protections from creditors' claims.

♦ Under changes made to the federal bankruptcy law in 2005, qualifying assets in 529 plans and Coverdell education savings accounts are protected in bankruptcy.[1]

---

1. Under the Bankruptcy Abuse Prevention and Consumer Protection Act of 2005, up to $5,000 in contributions made to a 529 plan between 365 days and 720 days prior to the filing of the bankruptcy petition, and an amount of contributions up to program limits for contributions more than 720 days prior, are excluded from the account owner's or contributor's bankruptcy estate. The account beneficiary must be the debtor's child, stepchild, grandchild, or step-grandchild.

If these programs are so great, why doesn't everyone know about them and use them?

The answer is that everyone *should* be aware of 529 plans, and in fact the word has been spreading. Surveys show that with each passing year more Americans gain familiarity with 529 plans. Over 13 million accounts now exist—an impressive number when you consider that nearly 2.5 million students will be graduating from high school in 2018 and enrolling in college the same year.[2]

Growth in 529 assets has also been impressive. At the beginning of 2002 there was approximately $14 billion in all 529 plans. This figure had increased to over $317 billion by the end of 2017. It is reasonable to expect continued rapid growth over the next few years.

What accounts for the popularity of 529 plans?

We can point to several factors:

- **Wide availability and full public acceptance of 529 plans.** Although several states have a tuition savings program dating back to the late 1980s, it was not until 1996 that Section 529 was added to the Internal Revenue Code, and the majority of programs now in operation are new since 1997. Except for Wyoming, every state has at least one 529 plan, many states have two, and a few have three or more. Educational institutions now have the authority to develop and offer their own 529 prepaid programs.
- **An outpouring of media interest** in 529 plans, particularly in the wake of the tax law changes in 2001 that granted a federal income-tax exemption for qualified distributions. Many personal finance periodicals, including *MONEY* and *Kiplinger's Personal Finance Magazine*, regularly mention 529 plans. Many of the country's top financial writers now recognize the advantages of 529 plans and recommend them

2. The *National Center for Education Statistics* estimates there will be 3.6 million new public high school graduates in 2017-2018, and in 2015 found that approximately 69.2 percent of high school students immediately enroll in college following graduation.

through their books, websites, public appearances, and newspaper columns.

♦ **Increased awareness of 529 plans among the professional investment and insurance community.** Before 2001, most brokers, investment advisors, and financial planners had little reason to promote 529 plans over other more traditional investment products because none of the state programs paid a commission. That has all changed now. Every segment of the professional planning community—hourly fee-based, asset fee-based, commission-based, or some combination—has a way to introduce 529 plans into its clients' portfolios and be compensated for their advice and guidance. For those individuals who wish to conduct their own research and make their own investment decisions while incurring lower fees and expenses, "direct-sold" 529 plans will be the preferred option.

♦ **Workplace enrollment.** Many employers are receptive to the idea of facilitating employee use of 529 plans by offering group enrollment and payroll deduction. As an after-tax voluntary deduction program, a workplace 529 program has no payroll tax implications, no discrimination testing, and few, if any, eligibility requirements. Hence, this additional "benefit" can be made available to employees at low or no cost to the company. Special considerations come into play, however, in deciding which particular 529 plan or group of plans to offer under a group-enrollment format. Since the dollars being contributed are coming from the employee, it is incumbent upon the employer to consider whether the 529 plans selected are the ones that offer the best benefits to their particular employees.

♦ **Private company affiliations.** An increasing number of private companies view higher education as a national priority and have recognized 529 plans as a way to help families that are facing the challenge of paying for college costs. Several of the customer loyalty programs have affiliated with 529 plans. By using particular credit cards or buying specific products, you earn "rewards" that can be automatically deposited into your 529 accounts. Upromise and Fidelity currently operate the largest rewards programs under formal agreements with 529 plans.

But don't 529 plans require that I send my child to an in-state public school?

This is one of the most common misconceptions about 529 plans. In fact, every state's 529 savings plan permits your account to be used at colleges and universities anywhere in the United States (and in many foreign countries as well). Some 529 plans provide better benefits for in-state schools, but none lock you into a specific institution or state public education system.

I've heard about the 529 plan in my state and it doesn't really excite me. That leaves me out, right?

Not at all. You should consider other states' programs. Many of the best 529 plans are operated by states that impose no residency restrictions. They are open to all.

I have already set up a 529 account in my state. So I guess I'm all set.

Guess again. Have you selected the program with the best benefits? If not, you may be better off rolling over your account to a different state's 529 plan. If a rollover is not a viable option (because of certain restrictions under federal law or the fees imposed by some 529 plans), you can leave your current account where it is and open a second account (or third account, etc.) with another state that offers a more attractive program.

My financial advisor tells me I am better off using his recommended mutual funds to save for college costs. Is he right?

Your advisor could be right, but it really depends on your particular circumstances and investment objectives. The better question is: How much does your financial advisor know about 529 plans? Until recent years, few were knowledgeable, and many felt threatened by the concept of a 529 plan, viewing it as a competitive product that provided little or no compensation. That situation has largely changed now that many states have approved commission-based 529 plans for distribution through broker-dealers. Financial professionals across the country, including commission-based advisors as well as fee-only planners, have begun embracing 529 plans as a potential solution for clients, and are finding ways to effectively incorporate them into long-term financial plans. Knowledge level remains the key, however. If you rely on a broker or financial planner in making investment decisions, be sure the advisor is up to speed on the technical and comparative aspects of 529 plans. A directory of financial professionals willing to work with college savers is available at Savingforcollege.com/find_a_529_pro.

My child is a senior in high school. Isn't it too late for me to start using a 529 plan?

Not necessarily. Assess your potential for tax savings by looking at your most recently filed income tax return. Did you pay any tax on interest, dividends, or capital gains distributions? If you did, a 529 plan represents an opportunity to convert taxable investment income into tax-free investment income. Even if the account has a life of only a few years—remember that it will usually take two to five years or even longer to earn a degree—you will be saving taxes. In fact, many parents facing college bills in the near future want to have their money in safe, interest-paying investments. This is the where the tax protection of a 529 plan provides the greatest advantage.

It gets even better if you live in a state that offers a state income tax deduction for contributions to a 529 plan. Instead of paying college bills out-of-pocket, you can reap the benefit of a state income tax deduction by first making a contribution to the 529 plan, and then using your account to pay the bills. Bottom line: college expenses become a write-off for state income tax purposes.

Section 529 plans sound too good to be true. Won't the IRS or Congress shut them down?

Not likely. Millions of American families are now investing in 529 plans and there is every indication that our elected officials in Washington want to see them become more popular, not less. This point was underscored at a June 2004 hearing held by the House Financial Services Subcommittee on Capital Markets. "The success of 529 tuition savings plans is good news," declared Rep. Michael G. Oxley in his opening statement. Since then, the federal government has passed several laws favoring 529 plans, including the Pension Protection Act of 2006 that made permanent the 529 tax exemption and the PATH Act of 2015 which expanded qualified expenses. In 2017, the Tax Cuts and Jobs Act further reinforced congressional support for 529 plans, by making up to $10,000 in private K-12 tuition a qualified expense.

There must be some disadvantages to 529 plans. What are they?

No single investment, including a 529 plan, is the perfect option for every investor. The advantages and disadvantages of 529 plans are discussed throughout this book. The fact that most 529 plans charge a fee to participants, as mentioned earlier in this chapter, is certainly one of the most obvious considerations. Here are some other significant disadvantages.

- Section 529 plans are confusing. It is not easy to feel comfortable with all the special rules and different options with 529 plans. There are plenty of places where you can learn about IRAs, savings bonds, and the like, and the rules for these programs are fairly uniform: one sponsor's IRA is not going to be much different from another. The same is not true for 529 plans. Rather than one basic model, there are several to choose from, and each 529 plan has unique features that make comparisons between different programs tricky. Many financial and legal advisors have not yet learned enough about the programs to effectively counsel their clients in this area. You can find quite a few helpful articles in the financial press, and the materials available from the programs themselves provide a great deal of useful information. In addition, the Securities and Exchange Commission and certain industry groups such as the Financial Industry Regulatory Authority (FINRA), Municipal Securities Rulemaking Board (MSRB), and the Securities Industry and Financial Markets Association (SIFMA) have put together explanatory booklets for the investing public. But apart from this book and the information on our companion website at www.savingforcollege.com, there is currently little comprehensive literature available from independent sources.

♦ The lower tax rates on capital gains and dividends do not apply to gains in your 529 account. Of course, if things work out right your earnings will be entirely tax-free, but if any part of a withdrawal turns out to be a nonqualified distribution, the earnings portion is taxable at ordinary income rates. There will also be a 10 percent penalty on earnings, unless you can apply one of the exceptions (see chapter 3).

♦ Investment selection in a 529 savings program is limited—although less so than in the past—and your ability to change investments is subject to restrictions. The ultimate responsibility for the investment and administration of your account rests with the state agency acting as trustee under the program trust. The state makes the rules, and the state can change the rules, provided the program continues to satisfy certain federal requirements. To date, most program changes have been beneficial to the participant but that may not always be the case.

♦ You may decide to invest with a particular 529 plan based in part on the program's selection of a particular mutual fund company or financial services firm as program manager, only to find that the program manager is replaced in a later year with a different investment firm. The contracts between the states and their outside program managers have terms lasting anywhere from two to 30 years, and at the end of the contract term a state can decide to bring in someone new. If that happens, it is likely that your account will have new investments and different expenses.

♦ The fact that you retain ownership and control over the account may work against you in certain situations. For instance, an account owner applying for Medicaid may find that the state Medicaid agency requires the 529 account first be used to pay for medical and long-term care expenses before Medicaid payments can begin. Or perhaps your 529 account is not eligible for special protections under state law or the federal bankruptcy law and a creditor attempts to reach your account for unpaid debts. These are risks you should discuss with your attorney.

♦ Your 529 account, and any distributions from it, can have an impact on the student's eligibility for need-based financial aid. However, depending on the relationship of the account owner and beneficiary, and the specific aid program in question, you may find the 529 plan treated much more favorably than alternative investment vehicles. This particular issue is covered in detail in chapter 4 and throughout the other chapters in this book.

I'm not sure I like the idea of the state holding my money. What's to prevent the state from appropriating the program funds for other purposes?

In most states, your contributions and account earnings are maintained in a separate legal trust that cannot be reached by the state for other purposes. If you have concerns about this, you should not hesitate to contact the program administrator in the state operating the program and obtain specific assurances.

My employer has recently started promoting a payroll deduction plan for college savings. Is this something I should consider?

Contributing to a 529 plan through payroll deduction can be a simple and relatively painless way to budget for college savings. Your employer may be interested in helping you learn more about the benefits of saving with a 529 plan and may even offer assistance in the enrollment process. Often the support and education is provided directly by a 529 program manager, or a financial advisor representing a 529 plan, under special arrangement with the employer. You will usually have the opportunity to attend special educational sessions, study program materials, and get your questions answered.

You should not assume that your employer's 529 plan is the best one for you. You will always have the option to establish an account on your own. Some employers will give you more choice by including two or more 529 plans on the payroll deduction platform. Employers will generally disclaim any responsibility for determining your suitability for the investment.

Contributions to a 529 plan through payroll deduction are made on an after-tax basis. Unlike a 401(k), your contributions are not subtracted from your taxable earnings, and they generally do not involve any payroll taxes or discrimination testing on the part of the employer.

I understand that 501(c)(3) exempt organizations can open accounts in 529 plans, but why would they want to?

Under the law, a charitable organization, or state or local government agency or instrumentality, opening a 529 account as part of a scholarship program is not required to name a beneficiary to the account, making it possible to establish the account now and select the scholarship recipients later on. Even with this flexibility, most scholarship-granting organizations will see little reason to use a 529 plan. They do not reap any benefit from the tax exemption under Section 529—charitable organizations do not pay tax on investment income anyway—and most have already established internal policies controlling the investment of their scholarship funds. However, organizations that do not currently have a scholarship program might be interested in starting one. The 529 plan makes available professional investment management and account administration at low cost. Many states and their program managers will be eager to facilitate the objectives of the scholarship program, including the processing of scholarship withdrawals to the institutions attended by scholarship recipients. There might also be valuable cross-promotional opportunities between the charitable account holder and the state. Students may prefer to receive scholarships through 529 plans because it minimizes potential for scholarship displacement. Scholarship displacement happens when a student's institutional need-based financial aid is reduced when they receive an outside scholarship. When a scholarship is awarded as a 529 plan contribution owned by the student or one of their parents, it is no longer considered cash support and will have a minimal effect on financial aid eligibility.

THREE

Section 529 Mechanics

This chapter describes the provisions of Section 529, including the tax benefits for the participant, the tax rules for distributions, and the various qualification requirements. It is a fairly technical chapter that includes information needed by the professional advisor who will be working closely with clients considering these investments.

Unfortunately, the amount of guidance coming from the Treasury Department and IRS has not been sufficient to address all the questions that can arise. Regulations are important because they interpret and supplement the tax law. The literal reading of the law must be coordinated with the practical demands placed on taxpayers.

The Treasury Department faces some particularly difficult issues in developing regulations under Section 529 due to the unique character of these programs. Proposed regulations were issued in August 1998, and were helpful at the time, but they became largely obsolete as a result of the Economic Growth and Tax Relief Reconciliation Act of 2001. More recently, the Pension Protection Act of 2006 gave Treasury increased authority to plug loopholes and prevent taxpayer abuse of Section 529 through regulations.

Meanwhile, we can look to other IRS documents for some help in applying Section 529. Notices, rulings, publications, and the tax forms along with their instructions provide direction but not a lot of detail. The best place for taxpayers to find official IRS guidance is Publication 970, Tax Benefits for Higher Education, available at www.irs.gov.

What is a 529 plan and who can participate?

A 529 plan is a program designed to help families prepare for the costs of elementary, secondary and postsecondary education that meets certain requirements contained in Section 529 of the Internal Revenue Code for a "qualified tuition program" or "QTP." Section 529 serves two basic purposes.

First, it prevents the IRS from challenging the tax-exempt status of the state-owned trust holding 529 assets. Without statutory protection, the trust could potentially be subject to income tax on its undistributed investment income.[1]

Second, Section 529 describes the federal income and transfer tax treatment of program participants. In some ways, the rules prescribed by Section 529 as they relate to participants directly contradict the "normal" rules under other provisions of the tax law.

Only two groups can offer a 529 plan. The first includes any state or state agency or instrumentality. The second includes any eligible educational institution. An institutional or "private" program could not be qualified under Section 529 prior to the 2001 EGTRRA changes, and in order to qualify now it must meet additional requirements and provide certain protections as discussed below.

A state-sponsored 529 plan is one that permits a person to either (1) purchase tuition credits or certificates on behalf of a designated beneficiary which entitle the beneficiary to the waiver or payment of his or

---

1. Trust earnings will not be considered "debt-financed income" for purposes of the tax on unrelated business income if the only liability of the program is to its participants.

her qualified higher education expenses or (2) make contributions to an account which is established for the purpose of meeting the qualified higher education expenses of the designated beneficiary.

The first type of program described in the preceding paragraph is commonly referred to as a prepaid program, while the second type is commonly referred to as a college savings program or college investment program. A savings program can be viewed as a kind of state-sponsored mutual fund—a participant's contributions to the program are invested and the value of the participant's account is determined by the investment performance of the underlying securities. It is not uncommon for the media to describe 529 plans as only referring to the savings programs.

In prepaid programs, the participant's "return" is not linked directly to investment securities. Some prepaid programs operate like futures contracts, where the participant purchases a contract that obligates the program to deliver a certain bundle of tuition or other benefits in the future, while others act like index funds, where the participant purchases redeemable units or credits whose value is pegged to average in-state public tuition or to some other tuition inflation index. In some significant ways, these unit-type prepaid programs have more in common with the savings programs than they have in common with the contract-type prepaid programs, and a couple of states have even relabeled their unit-type programs, replacing the word "prepaid" with the term "guaranteed savings."

An eligible educational institution that desires its own 529 plan is limited to offering a program that falls only into the first category, i.e. a prepaid program. In addition, it must hold its program assets in a "qualified trust," which is one that meets certain standards normally applicable to individual retirement accounts. The only such program currently in existence is the Private College 529 Plan.

When you establish an account in a 529 plan, you are required to name one living individual as designated beneficiary of the account. Typically, this is your child or grandchild, but it is not necessary that the beneficiary be related to you in any way. Multiple beneficiaries require multiple accounts. Most 529 plans permit you to name yourself as beneficiary of the account you establish.

Accounts established by a state or local government (or agency or instrumentality thereof) or by a 501(c)(3) exempt organization as part of a scholarship program are not required to name a designated beneficiary. Beneficiaries can be selected at the time of distribution, and one account can be used to assist multiple students in paying for college costs.

Almost anyone can participate in a 529 plan. There are no income or age limitations placed on either the account owner, the contributor (if different), or the designated beneficiary. There is no requirement that the participant reside in the sponsoring state or that the beneficiary attend a school located in that state. The 529 plan can establish its own restrictions, however, and so it is important to distinguish the flexibility permitted under federal law from the rules of the particular program you are considering.

What other requirements must a 529 plan meet?

All 529 plans must meet the following requirements in order to qualify under Section 529.[2]

1) The program can only accept contributions in cash, including check, money order, and credit card. Many 529 plans also permit electronic funds transfer from a bank or investment account. Contributions may not be made with investment securities or other types of property. To transfer other investments into a 529 plan you will need to liquidate those investments, possibly triggering taxable income or capital gains. Under certain conditions, you may be able to transfer funds from an existing Coverdell education savings account or qualified U.S. savings bonds without triggering tax. These rules are explained more fully in later chapters.

---

2. A state-sponsored 529 plan is not required to apply for a ruling or determination from the IRS as to its qualified status, although several states have requested, and some have received, such a ruling. An institution-sponsored program, however, is required to apply for and receive a determination from the IRS that it meets the requirements for qualification as a prepaid program under Section 529. At the time this book was published, only one institution-sponsored program, the Private College 529 Plan, had received such a determination from the IRS.

2) The program must provide a separate accounting for each designated beneficiary. Separate accounting does not mean separate investing, and contributions are typically commingled in the program trust for investment purposes.

3) The program may not permit you or your designated beneficiary to direct the investment of your account. The tax law is specific: investment direction must be left to the sponsoring state. Although this paternalistic provision appears to be very limiting, a savings program will in practice provide substantial investment choice and flexibility to the account owner. Nearly all programs now offer a menu of investment options. A contribution can be directed to one of these options, or in some 529 plans can be spread among the options (a small number of plans require that separate accounts be established if you want to invest in more than one investment option). You can request that your account be reallocated among the program's available investment options whenever you change the designated beneficiary, but if you maintain the same beneficiary you are limited to two such requests in any calendar year.[3]

4) The program may not allow accounts to be pledged by the account owner or designated beneficiary as security for a loan.

5) The program must provide adequate safeguards to prevent contributions on behalf of a designated beneficiary in excess of those necessary to provide for the qualified higher education expenses of the beneficiary. All 529 savings programs place a specific dollar limit on contributions, generally expressed as an account balance limit. An account balance limit means that a contribution will not be accepted by the program manager if the account value at the time of the intended contribution is above a specified level, although the account is not prevented from growing beyond that limit based on investment performance.

The IRS' 1998 proposed regulations provided a maximum-contribution safe harbor to programs that limit contributions on behalf of a

---

3. The 'Achieving a Better Life Experience Act of 2014' included a provision allowing an account owner of a 529 plan to change investment strategies twice per calendar year.

designated beneficiary to an amount determined by actuarial estimates necessary to pay tuition, required fees, and room and board expenses of the designated beneficiary for five years of undergraduate enrollment at the highest-cost institution allowed by the program. Most programs have abandoned the safe harbor and include graduate school costs and other qualified expenses in the computation of their contribution limits, presumably with assurances from the IRS or legal counsel that they will not jeopardize qualification under Section 529. (In a private letter ruling issued to New York's 529 savings program, the IRS approved a limit based on four years of undergraduate expenses and three years of graduate school expenses.) You will find many 529 plans with contribution account-balance limits in excess of $400,000 with a few over $500,000.

The limitation on contributions is imposed by the 529 plan on a per-beneficiary basis. If there is more than one donor to the account, or if there is more than one account in the program for a particular beneficiary, the accounts must be combined for purposes of determining total contributions. The IRS' proposed regulations did not, however, prohibit a designated beneficiary from maintaining accounts in different states and contributing a combined amount that exceeds the individual state limits. Congress presumably did not intend that the "stacking" of accounts be used as a way to circumvent the safeguards imposed by any one program, so it would be reasonable to anticipate that final regulations will impose additional requirements. Some states require a representation from the donor that accounts in multiple programs are not being used as a way to make contributions beyond the level that can be reasonably supported as appropriate for the beneficiary's future higher education needs.

I see some mutual fund companies advertising their own 529 plans. Can any investment firm offer a 529 plan?

No. The reason you see advertisements for 529 plans from mutual fund companies, broker-dealers, and banks is that many of the state-sponsored 529 plans have outsourced program management and marketing to these firms. Tax law requires that the state or institution "establish and maintain" the program but does not prohibit the sponsor from hiring a vendor to assume investment management and administrative duties. These vendors have a direct interest in the success of the programs, as their fees are typically based on the level of assets under management in the program. Under the 1998 proposed regulations, in order to meet its duty, a state must set all the terms and conditions of the program and be actively involved on an ongoing basis in the administration of the program, including supervising all decisions relating to the investment of assets contributed to the program.

What are the federal income tax rules for 529 plan participants?

Your contributions to a 529 plan are not deductible in computing your federal income tax. Your initial tax savings come from the deferral of income—earnings in your account remain tax-free until they are distributed. Distributed earnings may or may not be subject to tax, depending on whether the designated beneficiary incurs sufficient qualified higher education expenses (QHEE), as adjusted (AQHEE), during the year. QHEE and AQHEE are defined on page 12.

If you withdraw funds from your 529 account, or have payments made by the program to the beneficiary's school, the program administrator is responsible for sending Form 1099-Q to you or to your beneficiary after year-end reporting the gross distributions and breaking out the total between earnings and basis (return of principal). Distributions are always allocated pro-rata between earnings and basis. You will need the gross distributions and earnings figures when completing Form 1040, the federal income tax return. Basis always comes out federally tax-free.

If the account beneficiary has incurred AQHEE during the year that in total are equal to, or greater than, the total distributions from all 529 accounts as reported on Forms 1099-Q, the distributions are excluded from income and not reported on Form 1040. If, however, total AQHEE are less than total distributions, only a portion of the distributed earnings is excluded from income, and the remainder has to be reported as ordinary income. The calculation follows this formula:

$$\frac{\text{Gross Distributions} - \text{AQHEE}}{\text{Gross Distributions}} \quad \text{X} \quad \text{Earnings} \quad = \quad \text{Ordinary Income}$$

If withdrawals are made from a Coverdell education savings account for the same beneficiary during the year, QHEE must first be allocated between the 529 distributions and the Coverdell withdrawals. This is because withdrawals from a Coverdell ESA follow the same general taxation rules as distributions from a 529 plan. IRS Publication 970 suggests a pro rata allocation of expenses, but the IRS apparently will permit any other reasonable method. Coverdell ESAs are discussed in chapter 9.

A question that does not appear to be fully resolved is whether your payments for QHEE must match up with the distributions from your 529 account in the same taxable year. The timing of the transaction will not be a concern when the program makes qualifying payments directly to the school, but it can become an issue if you pay the college bills yourself. For example, let's assume you withdraw funds from your 529 account in December 2018 but wait until January 2019 to pay the tuition bill. A Form 1099-Q will be issued for 2018, but the tuition presumably counts as a 2019 expense, and you could end up paying tax and penalty because of the mismatch. This can also happen in the other direction. Let's assume you pay the tuition in late December and request a distribution from the 529 plan to reimburse yourself for the payment. If the distribution is processed in January of the following year, you potentially face a tax problem.

In Announcement 2008–17, the IRS announced that new regulations are expected to include a provision permitting qualified higher education expenses paid during the first three months of the year to be treated as the previous year's expenses. While this would eliminate the problem in the first scenario described above, it would not help with the second scenario (the reimbursement mismatch). Until further guidance is issued by the IRS, you should assume that QHEE and distributions will be accounted for on a cash basis and that 529 account distributions and the payment of qualified expenses must occur within the same calendar year.

Earnings subject to tax because they are part of a nonqualified distribution are also subject to a 10 percent federal additional tax. This tax, which represents the penalty for using a 529 account for purposes other than higher education expenses, is computed on Form 5329 as part of the Form 1040.

Note the following exceptions to the 10 percent federal additional tax:

♦ The distribution is made because the beneficiary is disabled—i.e., unable to engage in any substantial gainful activity because of a physical or mental condition and the condition is of indefinite duration or is expected to result in death.

♦ The distribution is made on account of tax-free scholarships or allowances received by the beneficiary, to the extent the distribution does not exceed the amount of scholarship or allowance.

♦ The distribution is made due to beneficiary's attendance at a U.S. military academy, to the extent the distribution does not exceed the costs of advanced education (as defined in Title 10 of the U.S. Code) at the academy.

♦ The distribution is paid to the beneficiary (or to the beneficiary's estate) on or after the death of the beneficiary.

♦ The distribution is included in income only because total qualified higher education expenses had to be reduced by tuition and related expenses used in computing the American Opportunity credit or Lifetime Learning credit.

How does the 529 plan administrator calculate the earnings portion of a distribution?

In producing Form 1099-Q, the 529 plan administrator first calculates the basis portion of the distribution and then subtracts that figure from the total distribution, leaving the earnings portion.[4] In a 529 savings program, the basis portion is calculated using the following equation:

$$\frac{\text{Basis}}{\text{Value of account}} \ \ \text{X Distribution} \ = \ \text{Basis portion}$$

---

4. Section 529 applies the provisions of Section 72 to the extent the distribution is not excludable under any other section of the Code (e.g. Section 117 scholarship exclusion).

Basis generally refers to the total contributions into the account less prior distributions of basis. The value of the account is determined on the day of distribution.

The calculation is slightly different in a prepaid program. The total amount of the distribution is the current value of the tuition and other education benefits your beneficiary receives during the year. The basis portion is calculated from the number of tuition credits used or redeemed during the year as a percentage of total credits purchased. For example, if you originally purchased eight semesters of tuition and you use the program to pay for two semesters in a year, the basis portion of the distribution is two-eighths or 25% of the amount you paid for the prepayment contract.

For purposes of these calculations, all 529 accounts within the same state with the same account owner and designated beneficiary must be treated as one account. Accounts in a prepaid program do not have to be aggregated with accounts in the same state's savings program.

Aggregation is performed by the 529 program administrator, and is not a responsibility of the taxpayer, which means that the administrator will need to track your account's basis over time in order to satisfy the distribution reporting requirements. Rollover contributions from another 529 plan, and tax-free transfers from Coverdell education savings accounts and qualifying U.S. savings bonds, pose a special challenge to program administrators because these transfers include untaxed earnings. (These types of transfers are discussed in further detail below and in later chapters.) The basis of contributions associated with these transfers must be adjusted for their untaxed earnings. IRS Notice 2001–81 prescribes the procedures a 529 plan must now employ to ensure that this information is properly recorded.[5]

The government's decision to make program administrators responsible for determining the basis and earnings portions of a distribution lifts some of the paperwork burden from your shoulders. You do not have to maintain your own tax basis records.

---

5. Notice 2001–81, 2001–52 IRB (Dec. 26, 2001).

Where do I show the beneficiary's qualified higher education expenses to the IRS?

You are not required to list or report the AQHEE on Form 1040 or any other income tax form. You must maintain records and be prepared to present those records in the event your return is audited by the IRS. If the distributions from a 529 plan are entirely excluded—AQHEE equal or exceed total distributions from Forms 1099-Q—no amounts need appear on Form 1040. If earnings must be reported—AQHEE are less than total distributions—they are to be included in "other income" on Line 21 of Form 1040.

Who reports any taxable earnings, the account owner or the beneficiary?

Form 1099-Q will be issued in the name and social security number of the recipient of the distribution (in tax parlance, the "distributee"). In most 529 savings programs, that can be either the beneficiary or the account owner. The recipient is responsible for the proper reporting of the distribution, and for any resulting tax (including the 10 percent additional tax). The account owner selects the recipient when filling out the program's withdrawal request form. Distributions paid directly from the 529 plan to the school are treated as paid to the beneficiary for reporting purposes.

Under the statutory language of Section 529, it appears that the designated beneficiary need only incur sufficient AQHEE for the distribution to be tax-free, no matter who receives the Form 1099-Q. If the parent, as account owner, receives the distribution (along with the Form 1099-Q), it should be excluded from the parent's income just as it would have been excluded from the beneficiary's income had the beneficiary received the distribution. However, because the Form 1099-Q contains a box that will indicate when the recipient is not the designated beneficiary, the account owner may have to deal with "matching" notices from the IRS and justify to the IRS the use of those funds to pay the designated beneficiary's college expenses. Future tax regulations should provide more clarity around this issue.

When the distribution is not a qualified distribution, you may have an opportunity to reduce taxes if the distribution is made payable to a low-bracket beneficiary.

Example: Mr. Brown establishes an account with a 529 plan for his daughter Kelly and makes a one-time contribution of $10,000. Five years later, once Kelly has started college and the account has grown to $15,000, Mr. Brown requests a $9,000 distribution from the account made payable to Kelly. Kelly will receive a Form 1099-Q after the end of the year showing $9,000 in total distributions with $6,000 as the basis portion and $3,000 as the earnings portion. The basis portion is two-thirds of total distributions, as determined by the ratio of the account's basis at the time of distribution ($10,000) to total account value ($15,000). If Kelly can show that she incurred at least $9,000 of adjusted qualified higher education expenses during the year, the entire distribution is federally tax-free. If Kelly can only show $5,000 of AQHEE, then 5/9ths of the $3,000 earnings portion will be tax-free and 4/9ths, or $1,333, will be subject to tax on Kelly's federal income tax return as ordinary income. She will also incur a 10 percent additional tax ($133).

What happens if the school issues a refund?

It is fairly common for payments of tuition or other qualified higher education expenses to be refunded in whole or in part by the educational institution. After paying the school bill, the student may drop credits, or drop out of school altogether. If the refund from the school is recontributed to the student's 529 plan within 60 days the distribution will avoid inclusion in income.

What about state taxes?

State tax laws are not uniform, but here, generally speaking, is the way it should work for most:

- Opening a 529 account in a state other than your own does not subject you or your beneficiary to that state's income tax.
- If a distribution qualifies for exclusion from federal taxable income, then it should also qualify for exclusion from your own state's taxable income. Currently, only one state—Alabama—will tax a qualified distribution, and only when that distribution comes from a non-Alabama 529 plan. Qualified distributions from an Alabama 529 plan remain exempt from that state's income tax. (The Alabama legislature has considered—but not yet passed—changes to its laws to remove this particular distinction.)
- If a distribution is federally taxable, then it will probably also be taxable on your state income tax return. You may also have to "recapture" any state tax deductions or credits claimed in previous years. Be careful here: some states will treat a federally tax-free rollover as a taxable distribution; and some states will exclude the income on a nonqualified distribution if the distribution is attributable to the beneficiary's death, disability, or receipt of a scholarship.
- Most states will follow federal rules regarding the amount and timing of reportable income, and concerning who reports it (account owner or beneficiary).

What are adjusted qualified higher education expenses?

Adjusted qualified higher education expenses (AQHEE) are qualified higher education expenses (QHEE) reduced by expenses used to claim an education tax credit. See the section below concerning the American Opportunity and Lifetime Learning credits for a description of this adjustment.

QHEE means tuition, fees, books, supplies, and equipment required for enrollment or attendance on a full-time or part-time basis at an eligible educational institution, plus, in the case of a "special needs beneficiary," any "special needs services."[6] In addition, QHEE includes room and board expense (both on-campus and off-campus) for students enrolled in eligible college programs on at least a half-time basis.[7] Effective January 1, 2018, the definition of QHEE was expanded to include up to $10,000 in K-12 tuition per beneficiary per year. The student's qualifying expenses must be reduced by any tax-free scholarships or payments, and by educational assistance allowances provided under certain federal programs.

QHEE under current law does not include the cost of transportation or personal expenses, even though they may be considered part of the "cost of attendance" for federal financial aid purposes. Repayment of student loans also does not qualify.

Eligible post-secondary educational institutions are defined by reference to Section 481 of the Higher Education Act of 1965 and include any accredited post-secondary educational institutions offering credit toward a bachelor's degree, an associate's degree, a graduate or professional degree, or another recognized postsecondary credential. Certain proprietary institutions and postsecondary vocational institutions also are eligible institutions. The institution must be eligible to participate in Title IV U.S. federal financial aid programs. To determine if a particular institution has

6. The definition of a "special needs beneficiary" has not yet been provided in Treasury Department regulations. The Conference Agreement to Act Sec. 401 of the 2001 EGTRRA references individuals who because of a physical, mental, or emotional condition (including learning disability) require additional time to complete their education.

7. The amount paid for room and board as QHEE cannot exceed (i) the allowance applicable to the beneficiary for room and board included in the "cost of attendance", as defined in section 472 of the Higher Education Act as in effect on June 7, 2001, as determined by the eligible educational institution for that period, or (ii) if greater, the actual invoice amount the beneficiary residing in housing owned or operated by the eligible educational institution is charged for room and board costs for that period. The room and board costs must be incurred during an academic period during which the student is enrolled or accepted for enrollment in a degree, certificate or other program (including a program of study abroad approved for credit by the eligible educational institution) that leads to a recognized educational credential awarded by an eligible educational institution. A student will be considered to be enrolled at least half-time if the student is enrolled for at least half the full-time academic workload for the course of study the student is pursuing as determined under the standards of the institution where the student is enrolled. The institution's standard for a full-time workload must equal or exceed a standard established by the Department of Education under the Higher Education Act.

been assigned a federal school code by the Department of Education, and presumably eligible under Section 529 as meeting these requirements, you may enter the name of an institution at the Department of Education's website at http://fafsa.ed.gov/FAFSA/app/schoolSearch. Many foreign universities are included on the list. Some states have requested that the IRS provide an official listing of eligible educational institutions, but so far none has been published.

When I tried looking up a particular school on the school code list I was not able to find it. Does that mean I cannot use my 529 plan for that school?

First, check to be sure you have correctly spelled the school's legal name on the look-up page. You can also request from that page a list of schools within a particular state or country, or click on "foreign" for a list of all international schools. If you still cannot locate a particular institution, contact the college, explain that you are trying to determine if the college is eligible under Section 529, and request that the college provide you with its federal school code. Although not every postsecondary institution is eligible, nearly all accredited institutions are.

> To see if an institution is 529 eligible, please visit Savingforcollege.com/eligible

Can I claim the American Opportunity or Lifetime Learning credit in the same year that I withdraw from my 529 account to pay for college?

Yes, the American Opportunity or Lifetime Learning credit (see box below) can be claimed regardless of whether the funds used to pay credit-eligible tuition and related expenses come from a 529 account. However, in order to prevent "double-dipping," Section 529 requires that QHEE be reduced by any expenses used to determine the American Opportunity or Lifetime Learning credit. Unless you pay out-of-pocket an amount at least equal to the amount of tuition and related expenses used in determining the American Opportunity or Lifetime Learning credit, some portion of your 529 distribution will no longer be qualified and will become subject to income tax. The 10 percent penalty tax will not apply in these circumstances.

> *Example:* Eric, a second-year college student, has his own 529 account. He withdraws $24,000 from the account during 2015 to pay for all of his QHEE, including $8,000 in tuition. The entire $24,000 distribution would be tax-free, except that Eric claims the maximum $2,500 American Opportunity credit against $4,000 of his tuition. He must reduce his $24,000 QHEE by $4,000, leaving $20,000. This means that $4,000 (or one-fifth) of his 529 distribution is no longer qualified. If we assume the earnings portion of the distribution is $5,000, then one-fifth of $5,000, or $1,000, is taxable to Eric as ordinary income. If Eric's marginal federal tax bracket is 15%, he incurs $150 in federal tax. The 10 percent penalty tax is waived when the income is caused by this type of adjustment.

You may elect to waive the American Opportunity and Lifetime Learning credit if you decide that its negative impact on 529 distributions is greater than the amount of credit. This will occur in only a very small number of cases because the benefit of the credit will nearly always outweigh the tax on that portion of your 529 distributions.

Note that similar coordination rules apply to withdrawals from a Coverdell education savings account. Furthermore, if withdrawals are taken from both a Coverdell ESA and a 529 account in the same year for the same beneficiary, the QHEE must be divided between them to determine the amount of tax exclusion on the withdrawals from each type of account. See chapter 9 for more information.

Tax Credits for Tuition Payments

The American Opportunity credit and the Lifetime Learning credit are available to taxpayers with incomes below a certain level who incur qualified tuition and related expenses. The Lifetime Learning credit is nonrefundable, so the amount you claim cannot be greater than your tax liability excluding the credits. However, as much as 40 percent of the American Opportunity credit is refundable to certain eligible taxpayers. You may elect to claim the credits by attaching Form 8863 to your original or an amended federal income tax return.

American Opportunity credit

The American Opportunity credit is equal to 100 percent of up to $2,000 of qualified tuition and related expenses paid by a taxpayer during the taxable year for the qualified educational expenses of a student during any academic period beginning in each taxable year, plus 25 percent of such expenses over $2,000. The maximum credit is $2,500 per year per student. The American Opportunity credit may be claimed up to four times. The student cannot have completed four years of postsecondary education before the start of the taxable year, and must be at least a half-time student.

For purposes of this credit, the term "qualified tuition and related expenses" means tuition and fees required for the enrollment or attendance of the taxpayer, the taxpayer's spouse, or any dependent of the taxpayer, at an eligible educational institution. Qualified expenses are reduced by tax-free scholarships and allowances.

The American Opportunity credit is phased out for taxpayers with modified adjusted gross incomes (MAGI) between $80,000 and $90,000 (single) or between $160,000 and $180,000 (married filing joint).

Lifetime Learning credit

The Lifetime Learning credit is equal to 20 percent of up to $10,000 of the qualified tuition and related expenses paid by the taxpayer during the taxable year for education furnished during any academic period beginning in the taxable year. The maximum credit is $2,000 per year per taxpayer (not per student). Tuition and related expenses for any course of instruction taken at an eligible educational institution to acquire or improve job skills of the individual are qualified. There is no limit to the number of years in which the Lifetime Learning credit can be claimed.

The Lifetime Learning credit is phased out for taxpayers with modified adjusted gross incomes (MAGI) between $57,000 and $66,000 (single) or between $112000 and $132,000 (married filing joint). These phase-out ranges are for 2017 and they adjust every year for inflation.

A taxpayer cannot claim an American Opportunity credit and a Lifetime Learning credit for the same student in one year. Also, any expenses used in determining the American Opportunity or Lifetime Learning credit will reduce total qualified higher education expenses used in calculating the tax exclusion for distributions from a 529 plan or Coverdell education savings account. Proper coordination and planning will maximize the benefits of these credits and exclusions over the course of a family's college years.

If you claim your child as a dependent, only you may claim the American Opportunity credit or the Lifetime Learning credit with respect to your child's qualifying educational expenses. Your child may claim the credit if you do not claim the child as a dependent on your tax return. (An otherwise dependent child cannot claim a personal exemption, however, no matter what the parent decides to do about claiming the dependency exemption.)

Your ability to decide whether to claim your child as a dependent provides significant latitude. If your income is above the limits, and your child's income falls below the limits, the child may derive a tax benefit from the credits when you cannot. You will lose the benefit of the dependency exemption, but some high-income parents are unable to derive full benefit from the dependency exemption anyway, due to the income phase-out of the exemption. In that case, you would make the easy decision to forego claiming your child as a dependent, and thereby allow the child to apply the education credit against his or her tax liability.

What are the federal gift and estate tax rules under Section 529?

Section 529 prescribes that the contribution to a 529 plan account is a completed gift for estate and gift tax purposes. The gift is from the individual contributor to the designated beneficiary (assuming the contributor and beneficiary are not the same person). This rule applies despite the fact the account owner retains ownership rights that would otherwise cause the assets to remain in his or her estate. A further advantage is that the funding of the account is treated as the gift of a "present interest" qualifying for the $15,000 gift tax annual exclusion. Finally, Section 529 provides that the contributor may under certain circumstances elect to treat the gift as occurring ratably over a five-year period, so that the $15,000 exclusion can be leveraged to as much as $75,000 in a year. Chapter 8 describes these rules in more detail.

Can I change the beneficiary of my 529 account?

Section 529 allows the account owner to replace the current designated beneficiary with a new beneficiary who is a "member of the family" (see box below). All 529 plans accommodate a change in beneficiary without imposing a penalty, although some may have age or residency restrictions, and some may charge a fee. There are no federal income tax consequences of a beneficiary change; however, there can be gift tax consequences when the new beneficiary is at least one generation below the old beneficiary, as discussed in chapter 8.

Can I transfer my account from one state's 529 plan to another state's 529 plan?

Yes, a qualifying rollover is not treated as a distribution for federal income tax. A transfer of assets from one state's plan to another for the same beneficiary is a qualifying rollover, but this type of rollover can be done only once every 12 months. There is no limit on the frequency of rollovers where the beneficiary is replaced with a qualifying member of the family. A rollover can be transacted either through a direct "trustee-to-trustee" transfer (program permitting), or by a withdrawal of funds followed by the contribution of equivalent funds within 60 days to a different 529 plan. Be sure to find out how the 529 plan you are investigating handles rollover requests, as there may be restrictions imposed by the program. Many prepaid programs will treat such a request as a cancellation of the contract.

Member of the Family

"Member of the family" means an individual who has one of the following relationships to the current beneficiary:

- ♦ A son or daughter (natural or legally adopted), or a descendant of either;
- ♦ A stepson or stepdaughter;
- ♦ A brother or sister (by whole or half-blood), or stepbrother or stepsister;
- ♦ The father or mother, or an ancestor of either;
- ♦ A stepfather or stepmother;

- A niece or nephew;

- An aunt or uncle;

- A son-in-law, daughter-in-law, father-in-law, mother-in-law, brother-in-law, or sister-in-law;

- The spouse of the designated beneficiary (who must have the same principal place of abode) or the spouse of any of the relatives listed above (who must have the same principal place of abode);

- A first cousin.

Can a corporation or trust be the owner of a 529 account?

Yes, Section 529 refers to a "person," defined under Section 7701 of the Code as an individual, a trust, estate, partnership, association, company or corporation. Many 529 plans permit legal entities to establish accounts, although some do not. There will be special tax considerations whenever a non-individual taxpayer is account owner, and some of the issues surrounding entity ownership have not been fully explored or tested. For corporations, the compensation rules (Section 83) must be considered, and perhaps also the anti-tax shelter provisions. For certain trusts, the effect of 529 plan distributions on "distributable net income" has to be considered. Your attorney and accountant should be consulted in these matters.

Can I transfer the ownership of my account to someone else?

Nothing within Section 529 prohibits or regulates a transfer of account ownership. It is up to the individual 529 plan to provide rules concerning transfer of account ownership. Some programs will accommodate a request to transfer account ownership while others expressly prohibit such transfers prior to the owner's death or legal incapacity. The mere transfer of ownership appears to have no federal income, gift, or estate tax consequences. However, a new account owner will generally have all rights associated with original ownership including the power to revoke the account.

What happens to my account if I die?

The death of the account owner does not cause a 529 account to terminate. Instead, all rights of ownership and control over the account are passed to a successor account owner. The identity of the successor owner depends on the rules of the program and state law. Nearly all 529 plans now permit you to name a successor owner on the account application or upon later submission to the program administrator. The program rules may specify the account owner in other situations, i.e. you fail to name a successor account owner, or the person you name as successor declines the appointment or predeceases you. For example, the 529 plan may specify that, in the absence of a named successor, the beneficiary of the 529 account will become account owner unless the beneficiary is a minor, in which case the beneficiary's living parent or guardian will become account owner. In any situation where there is no clear successor under the terms of your account or the rules of the program, ownership will pass according to your will or your state's laws of intestacy. If you live in a state with a community property law, consult with your attorney regarding the treatment of your 529 account.

FOUR

Financial Aid Considerations

We now turn our attention to one of parents' most significant concerns: the impact of a 529 account on a student's financial-aid eligibility. The news is positive, as the use of 529 plans to save for college under current rules causes little, if any, impact to a student's eligibility for need-based federal student aid. Non-federal awards may utilize different formulas that do not provide the same advantage to 529 plans. The aid process is explained below.

The authorization for federal financial aid comes from Title IV of the Higher Education Act of 1965, as amended (HEA). Financial-aid packages consist of any combination of grants, work-study, and loans. A student's financial need is determined by the institution as the difference between that particular institution's cost of attendance (COA)[1] and the student's expected family contribution (EFC). The EFC represents the amount the family is expected to contribute towards a student's college costs based on its financial situation.

---

1. COA includes tuition, fees, room and board, books, supplies, transportation, and personal expenses. Some institutions will choose not to include transportation and personal expenses in the COA figure.

The EFC is calculated using data submitted to the Department of Education on a form called the Free Application for Federal Student Aid (FAFSA). The FAFSA is filed by high school seniors after January 1 in their final year of high school. In subsequent college years, the student files an abbreviated Renewal FAFSA.

The EFC includes 50 percent of the student's income, net of an income protection allowance of $6,570 for the 2018–19 award year and allowances for federal, state, and social security taxes. It also includes 20 percent of the student's reportable assets.

For dependent students, the EFC also includes between 22% and 47% of the parents' income and between 2.64% and 5.64% of the parents' assets. The parents' income is reduced for this purpose by tax allowances and a maximum $4,000 employment expense allowance. The formula also provides "protection allowances," one for parental income based on the household census (e.g., for 2018–19 the income protection allowance when there are two parents and one student in the household is $22,810) and one for assets based on whether there is one parent or two and on the age of the older parent (e.g., the asset protection allowance for two parents with the oldest being 45 as of December 31, 2018 is $19,800).

The parental contribution to EFC is pro-rated to each member of the family attending college in the upcoming year. This pro-ration can have a dramatic effect and many families that would not qualify for financial aid with one student in college may qualify when they have two or more family members in college at the same time.

In completing the FAFSA, the applicant reports income for the base year, which is the calendar year two years prior to the start of the school year (e.g. 2016 is the base year for students enrolling in fall 2018). Income includes the adjusted gross income from the student's and parents' Forms 1040 along with certain other items representing "untaxed income and benefits." Assets are reported on the FAFSA at their values on the day the FAFSA is filed. Anyone attempting to position income and assets for improved aid eligibility should keep the timing rules in mind.

Special treatment is provided to low-income families where the student and parents were eligible to file Form 1040A or 1040EZ for the base year, or where they were not required to file any income tax return. The

EFC is automatically zero if the parents earned $25,000 or less. The "simplified needs" formula, which excludes assets but not income, applies if the parents earned more than $25,000 but less than $50,000.

Alternative needs formulas are used for independent students without dependents and for independent students with dependents. A student is automatically considered independent if he or she is at least 23 years old, a veteran of the armed forces, a master's or doctoral candidate, married, or declared independent by a court, or if he or she has legal dependents other than a spouse. Parent assets and income are not considered in the need analysis for these students. The Department of Education maintains an extensive library of publications and other materials relating to federal financial aid on the Web at www.ed.gov.

> **You can estimate your financial aid eligibility by visiting Savingforcollege.com/FinAid**

Does all need-based aid come from the federal government?

No, most states also maintain need-based grant programs. Many of these programs use the federal methodology in determining the student's need while others use state-developed criteria. In some states, the determination of student eligibility for state-funded programs does not count balances in the home-state 529 plan. This can be an incentive to use your state's own 529 plan.

Many institutions, primarily private colleges, provide substantial amounts of gift aid out of their own endowments and other funds. A large number of these colleges utilize an alternative approach in determining need known as the "institutional methodology," developed by the College Board and administered by its affiliate, College Scholarship Service (CSS). To apply for grants at colleges that use the institutional methodology, a student must complete an application called the PROFILE. The PROFILE is similar to the FAFSA in that it follows the same general approach and is used to compute the applicant's expected family contribution. But there are also many differences between the forms, some of which are significant. For example, the PROFILE application requires information about equity in the home and family farm, which are exempt assets under the federal methodology. It will also provide information to the financial aid administrator about any retirement accounts owned by the student. The rest of this chapter focuses primarily on the federal methodology, not the institutional methodology; as you read through it, keep in mind that the treatment of 529 plans can differ. If your child will be applying for financial aid at a college using the institutional methodology, you should contact the college's financial aid office to determine its policies surrounding 529 plans.

Does the federal methodology distinguish between Section 529 prepaid tuition programs and savings programs?

No, although it used to. Before 2006, prepaid tuition plans caused a dollar-for-dollar reduction in need-based awards, but beginning with the 2006–07 award year, all 529 plans are treated the same in the determination of the student's EFC. As opposed to a 529 savings account, the value of a participant's interest in a prepaid tuition plan is not tied to the value of a portfolio of investments. Instead, the FAFSA requires that tuition credits or certificates purchased in a prepaid tuition plan be reported at their refund value.

How are 529 plans treated in the federal aid formula?

A 529 account owned by a dependent student's parent is reported on the FAFSA as a parent asset and assessed in determining the EFC at the parent's rate, which can be no higher than 5.64 percent, depending on income. If the account is valued at $10,000 on the day the FAFSA is filed, the maximum impact on aid eligibility is $564.

However, a 529 account owned directly by the dependent student, or owned indirectly through an UTMA/UGMA, is NOT reported as a student asset. Rather it is included with parent assets. This is good news as the assessment rate on student assets—at 20 percent—is significantly higher. This favorable treatment for student-owned 529 accounts—also applicable to Coverdell education savings accounts—came about under a change in federal law intended to encourage college savings by minimizing the negative impact on financial-aid eligibility. Prior to 2006, a student-owned 529 account was assessed like any other student-owned investment at the 35 percent rate then in effect for student assets. (For school years beginning in 2006, 2007, and 2008 the financial-aid laws contained an unintended loophole that effectively exempted student-owned 529 accounts from being reported on the FAFSA.)

Three other possible situations merit special attention:

- First, if the 529 account owner is the grandparent or another third party, it is not reportable on the FAFSA. This may sound like good news, but be sure to read the discussion below concerning "untaxed income."
- Second, if the 529 account owner is a legal trust established for the student's benefit, the special exception for student-owned 529 account described above presumably does not apply and the student's interest in the trust, including any applicable portion of the 529 account, will have to be reported as a student asset.
- Third, the FAFSA must include as a parent asset the value of a 529 account the student's parent owns for someone else, such as a younger sibling. This result can be avoided by placing the ownership of the account in the name of the sibling or a custodian under the UTMA/UGMA, but most parents would not wish to transfer ownership and control of the account for what is likely a very small impact on financial-aid eligibility.

Should we be transferring assets out of mutual funds and into a 529 plan to improve our child's eligibility for financial aid?

If the mutual fund is currently in a UGMA/UTMA account or in the student's name directly, you should look into the possibility of transferring the money to a 529 plan, as you would be converting a 20 percent asset to a 5.64 percent asset. The transfer of a $10,000 investment, for example, could increase financial aid eligibility by as much as $1,436.

However, you need to weigh the consequences of liquidating the non–529 investments (a 529 plan can only accept cash). By triggering capital gains you are creating an immediate income tax liability, and if the gains are reportable to your child under the age of 24, the kiddie tax may require those gains to be taxed at your (the parent's) higher bracket. The reporting of gains on your tax return, or on your child's tax return, will also be included in the base-year income on the FAFSA filed in the following year, thereby reducing aid eligibility.

If you are the parent of a dependent student and the mutual fund is in your name, there is no longer any financial-aid advantage in moving the funds to a 529 with your child as owner. Either way, the account value will be included on the FAFSA as a parent asset.

Placing your college savings in a 529 plan can help you qualify for zero- or simplified-EFC status because the 529 plan will not cause you to report capital gains. If you or the student were to invest in mutual funds or other securities, any gains from the sale of those securities would require that you file Schedule D with your Form 1040, thereby disqualifying you from special EFC status.

Are the distributions from a 529 plan reportable as "untaxed income" on the FAFSA?

Tax-free distributions from a 529 savings account owned by the student or parent do not constitute untaxed income and, therefore, will not impact the EFC. This can provide a tremendous advantage to 529 plans as compared with mutual funds, municipal bonds, or other investments that generate reportable interest, dividends, or capital gains.

With respect to distributions from 529 accounts owned by grandparents or other third parties, the answer is decidedly different. Although a provision in the 2007 College Cost Reduction Act prevents such distributions from being treated as a "resource" that reduces financial need on a dollar-for-dollar basis, the distribution will have to be included in base-year student income on the FAFSA line that asks for "Money received, or paid on your behalf (e.g. bills), not reported elsewhere on this form." This result can be avoided by waiting until the year in which the student enters his or her junior year of school before taking distributions from a grandparent-owned 529 (assuming they will graduate in four years). A grandparent can also consider transferring 529 account ownership to the parent or student if the money is needed sooner.

How does a 529 account compare to ESAs and IRAs?

Beginning in 2006, Coverdell ESAs and 529s are treated alike in the federal financial-aid formula. An ESA for a dependent student is reported as a parent asset, and tax-free ESA distributions are not reportable as untaxed income.

In comparing a 529 plan to a traditional or Roth IRA, special care is needed. Although an IRA is generally considered to be a favored type of investment when it comes to the financial-aid formula, it may in fact have severe negative financial aid consequences to the unsuspecting family. Qualified retirement accounts, including IRAs, are excluded assets in the EFC computation and, as discussed in chapter 11, premature distributions from an IRA may now be taken penalty-free to pay for college. The problem is with the income side of the EFC computation. The entire amount of the IRA distribution—both principal and earnings–is reportable on the FAFSA. Aid-eligible families with retirement assets should not plan on tapping those accounts to pay for college until the year in which the last FAFSA is filed.

Of course, many families will never expect to qualify for financial aid regardless of who is credited with the assets and income. For them, the financial-aid implications of a 529 plan, or any other investment alternative, will be of little concern. Even those who do qualify may discover that financial aid means loans and work-study, not grants or scholarships. Their concerns about the financial-aid consequences of investment decisions should also be tempered.

Federally-Funded Student Aid

- **Federal Pell Grants**—Non-discretionary grants awarding up to $6,095 for the 2018–19 award year to applicants with financial need.

- **Federal Supplemental Educational Opportunity Grants** (FSEOG)—Up to $4,000 per year allocated by the institution to students with financial need.

- **Federal Stafford (Direct) Loans**—Student loans directly from the government available to all students, but subject to annual borrowing caps. Limited interest subsidy is available to students determined to have financial need.

- **Federal Direct PLUS Loans**—Similar to Stafford, but made to creditworthy parents of students. Also available to graduate students.

- **Federal Perkins Loans**—Up to $5,500 per year ($8,000 for graduate study) of 5%-interest loans allocated by the institution on the basis of financial need.

- **Federal Work-Study** (FWS)—Funds provided by government for an institution's part-time employment of students with financial need.

You can see how much of an impact saving for college can have on future student loans by visiting Savingforcollege.com/loans

FIVE

Prepaid vs. Savings

Section 529 plans come in two basic forms: prepaid and savings. But categorizing any given program is not always simple. Some plans contain features that are common to both prepaid and savings programs. They act like a prepaid program under some conditions, and like a savings program under different conditions. Some states even combine their separate prepaid and savings programs into a single package, marketed to the public as one program with different options.

If your state operates a prepaid program, one of your first steps should be to check whether the program is accepting new enrollments. Several states, including Alabama, Colorado, Illinois, Kentucky, Ohio, South Carolina, Tennessee, and West Virginia have temporarily or permanently suspended enrollment into their prepaid programs. Other states may follow suit if program financial solvency is further stressed by rising tuition levels.

What is a prepaid program?

A prepaid program is one involving the purchase of tuition credits or certificates that entitle the beneficiary to a waiver or payment of future qualifying college costs. In essence, future tuition is being purchased today. The price you pay now is not necessarily equal to current tuition levels, although current tuition is always a factor when a prepaid program establishes its prices.

There are three types of prepaid programs. The most prevalent is the state-sponsored **"contract" program**. In return for your upfront cash payment, or your commitment to a series of cash payments, you receive a promise from the program that it will pay for future tuition and mandatory fees at public colleges, universities, or community colleges located in the state. The contract may cover a period from one semester to five years, depending on the program's available packages and the amount of tuition you wish to purchase. If your beneficiary attends a private or out-of-state school, the program will determine the value of your contract under a preset formula and make payments in an amount not to exceed that value.

The second type of prepaid program, also state-sponsored, is a prepaid/savings hybrid that is sometimes referred to as a **"unit" program**. It typically involves the purchase of tuition units or credits that represent a fraction (e.g. 1%) of the average yearly tuition and mandatory fees at public institutions in the state. These units change in value each year as average in-state tuition and fees increase. They are redeemed in the future to pay for tuition and fees, and in most cases, they can be redeemed for other qualified expenses as well (room and board, books, supplies, and equipment).

Categorizing the unit program as either prepaid or savings remains a matter of debate; it makes little difference now that prepaid programs and savings programs are treated equally in determining student eligibility for federal financial aid (see chapter 4). In 2000, a time when prepaid programs were at a severe disadvantage in the federal formula, Pennsylvania reconfigured its unit-type prepaid program in an effort to secure more favorable treatment for its participants, and labeled it a "guaranteed savings" program.

The third type of prepaid program, referred to here as a **"voucher" program**, involves the voluntary participation of one or more educational institutions. In return for your contribution, you receive a certificate redeemable toward a specific percentage of tuition and mandatory fees at any of the participating institutions. Percentages are set at the time of contribution. For example, the program may provide that a $5,000 contribution is worth 50 percent of one year's tuition and mandatory fees at participating College A, and 30 percent at College B. If your child attends one of those participating institutions, the tuition bill is reduced by the stated percentage. If your child attends a non-participating institution, or decides not to go to college at all, you can request a return of your payments adjusted for interest or other factors as described in program materials.

The Massachusetts U.Plan, with over 80 Massachusetts private and public institutions, was the first to offer a voucher-type prepaid program. The U.Plan is not a true 529 plan, but because it involves the issuance of Massachusetts general obligation bonds, participants are not subject to federal and Massachusetts state income tax. Another pure voucher-type program is the Private College 529 Plan, the private-college prepaid program that launched in fall 2003.

Here is another way to think about the three different types of prepaid programs: A contract program works like a futures contract; a unit program like an index fund (the index being average tuition at selected schools); and a voucher program like a discount coupon. All three rely on the program trust fund, made up of participant payments or contributions, to generate an investment return sufficient to cover the program's liability—or in some cases, the school's liability—for future tuition payments and unit redemptions.

What is a savings program?

A 529 savings program is a more familiar type of tax-deferred investment, in several ways similar to a Roth IRA. Contributions are made to a trust fund that is invested in mutual funds and other financial instruments. The idea is that your account will grow in value over time to keep up with, or preferably surpass, the increasing price of a college education.

Before Congress enacted Section 529 in 1996, several states had prepaid tuition programs but only one state, Kentucky, had a pure savings program. Since 1996, a majority of the new 529 plans are savings programs. There appear to be a couple of reasons for this phenomenon. One is that savings programs offer the potential for higher investment returns than prepaid or guaranteed savings programs. Accounts are usually invested in equity and bond mutual funds that have historically outpaced the increases in college expenses.

The other reason is that savings programs are easier and cheaper for a state to administer, especially when the outside vendor that manages the investments also agrees to handle much of the program administration and marketing. In recent years, several states have launched new or redesigned programs in which the program fund is charged a fee that is shared by the program manager and the state treasury, in effect making the program a source of revenue for the state.

What are the major differences between prepaid and savings programs?

Most people evaluating college-savings plans will, quite naturally, focus attention on the investment aspects of the programs being considered. After all, we all want our investments to do as well as possible. Historically, over long periods of time, stocks have outperformed many other investments, and certain types of common stocks have done better than others. On the other hand, stocks generally carry more investment risk than most other types of investments.

Nearly all 529 plans, of either variety, employ professional investment managers to maximize potential return within a certain level of risk. In a savings program, the investment management is applied directly to the assets in a participant's account. In a prepaid or guaranteed savings program, the investment management is applied to the program fund to ensure that the program will be able to pay for future tuition or unit redemptions. Because a participant will have no choice in the state's selection of investment managers, the participant must rely on the judgment of program officials.

While most savings programs offer the advantage of unlimited upside investment potential, prepaid and guaranteed savings programs offer the advantage of keeping up with inflation of college expenses, no matter how high those costs may go. A risk-tolerant saver may be more attracted to the savings program while a risk-averse saver may be more attracted to the prepaid or guaranteed savings program.

Here are some of the major differences between prepaid and savings programs:

1) In a savings program you own an interest in the program fund by virtue of your contributions into that fund. Your contributions are co-mingled with those of other participants, but the program administrator keeps track of each dollar you put in by setting up a separate account for you. With a prepaid program, you are purchasing the program's promise to deliver an agreed-upon bundle of benefits in the future. The amount you pay for that promise is determined by the program, as is the amount of any refund you may request later on. You should attempt to compare the price of the prepaid contract to the current tuition and fee levels at the institution your beneficiary is likely to attend. Is it the same, higher, or lower? Most state-sponsored prepaid programs are now charging more than the amount you would pay if your beneficiary were attending college this year. This "premium" is necessary for the program to cover administrative costs as well as to help build a reserve against potential shortfalls in the trust fund. A shortfall can occur if the program's obligation for future payments increases faster than the investment earnings in the trust. A premium causes the overall return of your investment in the prepaid contract to be somewhat less than the rate of tuition inflation. The price of the contract may also vary based on the age of your beneficiary. Prepaid programs often offer lower prices for younger beneficiaries because a longer time horizon allows for more predictable investment returns in the program trust fund.

2) Most prepaid programs have a specified enrollment period each year. Prepayment contracts must be purchased during the enrollment period, and the price of a contract is adjusted each year when the new enrollment period begins. Alternatively, some prepaid programs are now permitting year-round enrollment but setting new prices at certain times during the year. Savings programs do not have restricted enrollment periods and accept new accounts and contributions at any time.

3) Almost all state-sponsored prepaid programs require that either the account owner or the beneficiary meet state residency requirements. The majority of savings programs, however, are open to residents of any state. Any

family considering investing in a 529 plan should evaluate programs from the state where the donor lives, from the state where the designated beneficiary lives, and from states that offer 529 plans without residency requirements.

4) Most prepaid contracts are of limited duration. For example, the program may specify that the contract will be terminated, and a refund paid, if the benefits are not used within 10 years after the beneficiary's normal college matriculation date. Most savings programs, however, have no program-imposed limit on account duration and can remain open indefinitely, subject only to the requirement that there be a living beneficiary named on the account.

5) Most contract-type and voucher-type prepaid programs provide only for undergraduate tuition and mandatory fees, while savings programs and unit-type prepaid programs can generally be used for any costs that meet the definition of "qualified higher education expense" under Code Section 529. Unless the student is commuting from home, tuition and fees comprise less than 50 percent of the student's total cost of attendance at most in-state public institutions. However, nothing prevents a family from combining participation in a prepaid program with participation in a savings program.

6) All 529 plans allow distributions to pay for out-of-state colleges and universities. However, contract-type prepaid programs are generally designed for the child who eventually will be enrolling at an in-state public institution. For the beneficiary in a prepaid program who attends an in-state private school or an out-of-state school, the contract benefits must first be valued. Many programs use the weighted-average, credit-hour value of in-state public universities for this purpose. However, some prepaid programs compute a value by adding a fixed rate of interest to the contract purchase price. Also, most of these programs will limit the benefits paid to private and out-of-state institutions to the lesser of actual tuition and fees or the value of in-state tuition and fees. This means that a participant who moves out-of-state and then attends a public university in the new state will not receive a refund if the new state has lower in-state tuition than the old state. In this situation, the best move may be to cancel the contract and obtain a refund. The choice of college is not an issue in most savings and unit-type prepaid programs because beneficiaries receive

the same amount whether they attend an in-state public, an in-state private or an out-of-state school.

7) Even if the beneficiary of a contract-type prepaid program chooses to enroll in an in-state public institution, the investment return will often depend on the institution attended and the number of credit hours taken. A student attending the most expensive public university in the state and taking the maximum number of credit hours covered under the contract receives a better deal than the student who attends the least expensive university or takes fewer credit hours than the program is obligated to cover. In some states, the range of tuition prices among public institutions is wide. The ultimate choice of school does not affect the investment return in a savings program or unit-type prepaid program.

8) Most prepaid programs make payments directly to the institution after receiving notice of pending tuition bills from the participant. Savings programs generally permit cash withdrawals by the account owner or beneficiary, and do not require documentation to substantiate the use of the withdrawn funds. (Some savings programs will ask on the withdrawal request form if the withdrawal is "qualified" or "nonqualified." The participant's response is not determinative for federal tax purposes.)

9) State-sponsored prepaid programs tend to have more transaction fees than savings programs. Perhaps this is because prepaid programs are more difficult to administer, or because they are operated by state agencies that are accustomed to imposing fees. All 529 plans will list the fees charged to participants, including fees for enrollment, annual maintenance, and change of beneficiary or account owner. Savings programs compete more directly with other investment alternatives available to the college saver, and seem more intent on keeping fees and transaction charges to a minimum.

10) Some prepaid programs require a minimum purchase of at least one semester's worth of tuition, but allow payments to be made over time. The installment payments include an interest component, although the full payments are included in the tax basis of the account and none of the extra payment is treated as interest expense for income tax purposes. Savings programs do not work this way and simply credit the account whenever a contribution is received.

11) State-sponsored prepaid programs, including both the unit-type and guaranteed savings programs, make actuarial assumptions in evaluating the soundness of the program trust fund and in setting prices for the upcoming enrollment period. Relevant factors used to calculate the liability for future payouts include the projected investment return on fund assets, tuition increases and enrollment trends at state schools, and the expected number of refunds. Although the bull market of the 1990s allowed several prepaid programs to build up large reserves, stock market losses and spiraling public tuition in subsequent years created significant financial challenges for many of these programs. Reserves began drying up and by the end of 2002 nearly all prepaid programs were showing deficits on their balance sheets. The financial situation was particularly difficult for newer prepaid programs that opened in the midst of the financial squeeze. This situation was repeated during the 2008-09 recession. Several states closed off their prepaid programs to new enrollment, and will reopen only when financial conditions improve or when the programs can be restructured to minimize the risk of loss.

12) Some prepaid programs and unit-type programs are backed by the full faith and credit of their sponsoring states, providing a safety net for participants should the program run out of funds. A few programs do not enjoy this guarantee, but do offer some added safety under laws that require their state legislatures to consider an appropriation if their 529 plan runs into financial difficulties. Still other programs have no backing or guarantees from the state whatsoever, although the ongoing commitment on the part of the state may be implied. Savings programs typically have no state guarantee, and should have no reason to need one.

It is reasonable to expect that over time we will see further blurring of the lines that distinguish prepaid and savings programs. We are already beginning to see savings programs offering some inflation-protection features normally associated with prepaid programs, including guaranteed investment options. At the same time, some prepaid programs are becoming more flexible and investment-oriented. It may be difficult to achieve, but there is no reason why the best features of each type of 529 plan cannot be successfully incorporated into a single program.

SIX

Comparing 529 Plans: A Checklist

Beyond the basic characteristics of the two types of 529 plans described in the previous chapter, numerous differences exist in program design among the various programs operating today. The task of sorting through all the choices can be somewhat daunting. Just understanding how the 529 plan in your home state works is difficult enough; shopping among competing 529 plans becomes even more confusing.

Your analysis should involve not only a comparison of each program's investments or tuition guarantees, but also many other aspects of the program. Your own family circumstances, investment objectives, risk tolerance, and financial knowledge will all play a large part in selecting an appropriate 529 plan. The "best" 529 plan for one family is not necessarily the best one for another.

How do you go about this selection process? This book and our companion website (www.savingforcollege.com) are certainly good first steps. Then be sure to obtain the official program materials for your own state's 529 plan. Finally, request information from other states' programs that interest you and that accept nonresidents.

Many individual investors rely on a professional financial planner or investment advisor in developing, implementing, and monitoring an investment plan. Before 2001, few financial professionals had the knowledge, experience, and interest in 529 plans to be of much help to you in this regard. But over the past twelve years, professionals have awakened to the benefits of 529 plans for their clients, and many programs have been adapted for sale through financial advisors.

Whether you use a financial advisor to help select a 529 plan, or search on your own, learn as much as you can about the program before you invest in it. Here are the primary information sources that may or may not be included in the materials that a program makes available to you:

State statute. Every state with a 529 plan will have a law on the books authorizing the program. Sometimes, more than one section of state law is involved, e.g., when special state tax treatment is provided for participants in the 529 plan.

Program rules. Usually, a state agency or program board is charged with implementing and overseeing the operation of the program and acting as trustee. This agency develops the official rules of the program as allowed by the statute. These rules are extremely important because they contain the program's operational details. The rules are prone to frequent change, however, so it is important to be sure that you are accessing the most current version.

Program description. All 529 plans now provide an extensive explanatory booklet that describes their rules. This document also explains the tax treatment of 529 accounts and contains appropriate disclaimers.

Investment prospectuses. If a 529 savings program invests in mutual funds, it may send you the prospectuses for those funds—the same SEC-registered prospectuses that any investor would receive. The 529 plan itself is not required to produce a prospectus because securities laws treat interests in a 529 plan as "municipal securities" exempt from Securities and Exchange Commission registration requirements.

Program booklet. You will usually find an attractive, glossy marketing piece that contains pictures of cute children and summarizes the key advantages of the program. This is often presented in a helpful FAQ (frequently asked questions) format. An enrollment/application form is generally provided with the program booklet.

Website. Every 529 plan has a website. The Internet has become an extremely important and useful way to convey information and is perfectly suited to these programs. The best websites will make available all the materials provided in the enrollment packet, plus higher-education information including college-cost calculators and links to state financial-aid programs. Many 529 plans now allow you to enroll on-line.

The remainder of this chapter describes many of the ways in which 529 plans may differ from one another, and suggests an approach for comparing the various programs. This approach takes the form of a three-step process:

Step 1: Eliminate any 529 plans that clearly fall outside your criteria for acceptability, as well as those that will not accept you due to their eligibility requirements.

Step 2: For each program being considered, ask yourself the question "How much will my invested dollar produce by the time my beneficiary will need the funds to pay tuition?" Your own investment objectives, K-12 or college education plans, and risk tolerance will play a part here. Be sure to consider the level of fees and expenses, as well as any state-tax benefits and other financial incentives offered by the plan.

Step 3: If Step 2 does not produce a clear winner in your mind, make a comparison of the restrictive features in the programs. For example, some programs permit your relatives to make contributions directly to your account, while other programs do not. This feature may or may not be important to you; that is for you to decide. You can often circumvent a restriction by using multiple 529 plans, or by rolling over your 529 account to a less-restrictive 529 plan later on.

How much time will you need to complete this three-step process? It could be a lot, depending on how many possibilities you wish to explore. There are so many 529 plans to choose from and they differ in so many ways that your beneficiary could have completed college before you finally complete the exercise. That would not be a good thing. The tools available in this book, i.e., the checklist in this chapter and the online tools and information available at www.savingforcollege.com/bestwaytosave, can help shortcut the process.

Before making any final decisions, however, read and understand the official program materials of the programs you are most interested in. Contact the program administrators directly to obtain further explanation and clarification. For some important items (e.g., legal and tax questions), consider having a conversation with your attorney, accountant, or other professional advisor. The importance of a thorough due-diligence process cannot be overstated because it can greatly reduce the chances of being surprised or disappointed later on.

The following checklist is presented in three sections. It is organized in this manner so that you may more easily identify the 529 plans most likely to meet your needs. Revisit this checklist occasionally, as 529 plans are constantly making changes—usually improvements—to their program rules and investment options. Please note that this checklist excludes items that pertain exclusively to prepaid tuition programs. Please refer to chapter 5 for a discussion of how to compare features in prepaid plans.

> To quickly and easily compare different 529 plans, please visit Savingforcollege.com/compare

Section 1: Required elements

The first section describes eligibility or user requirements that either the program or the investor may impose when determining program suitability. As you read through these, remember that certain items will be viewed as requirements by only some investors. For other investors, they may have no relevance or importance.

1) Are there any state residency requirements?

Most 529 savings programs do not require that you or the designated beneficiary reside in the sponsoring state, but a few do. Conversely, 529 prepaid programs generally restrict enrollment to those who meet state residency requirements. Of course, the Private College 529 Plan does not have state residency restrictions, because it is not state-run. The Massachusetts U.Plan is a non-529 prepaid program that accepts anyone who intends to send their child to a participating Massachusetts college or university.

Often, a 529 plan with restrictions will permit enrollment if either the account owner or the beneficiary is a state resident at the time of enrollment. If you are establishing an account for a grandchild living in a different state, you may want to consider the program offered in the state where your grandchild resides.

Questions regarding residency can arise in certain situations. Is there a minimum period of residency? What happens if the eligible resident moves out-of-state after the account is opened? What happens if enrollment is contingent on the state residency of the beneficiary, and you later change the beneficiary to someone who is not a state resident? How are the residency restrictions applied to military personnel stationed in the state, or those originally from the state but now stationed elsewhere?

Some 529 plans that impose residency restrictions will accept nonresidents who meet other conditions. For example, Nevada's prepaid program allows a nonresident alumnus of a Nevada postsecondary institution to enroll.

2) What are the other eligibility requirements?

Most 529 plans require that the individual account owner be of legal age (e.g. 18) and that an account funded with a minor's own money be maintained by an adult custodian or guardian on behalf of the minor. In addition, the program may be restricted to account owners who are U.S. citizens or resident aliens. The program may require that the beneficiary have (or obtain within a certain period of time) a Social Security number or a federal taxpayer identification number.

Most prepaid programs require that the beneficiary be below a certain age or grade level at the time of enrollment, making these programs unsuitable for older individuals who may be planning to attend college in the future.

3) Can the account owner and the beneficiary be the same person?

Although every 529 savings program permits you to establish an account for yourself, this may not always be feasible in programs that place age or grade limits on beneficiaries. Such restrictions are common in prepaid programs.

4) How does the program handle funds coming from an existing UTMA or UGMA investment account?

Many families have children with assets in a Uniform Transfers to Minors Act (UTMA) account or Uniform Gifts to Minors Act (UGMA) account. If you are the custodian of the account, and you wish to invest the child's assets in a 529 plan, you will need to determine if, and how, the program accommodates funds coming from UTMA/UGMA accounts. There are a few different ways this is being done.

- ◆ The program (e.g. New York) will permit the minor child to establish an account in his or her own name. A parent or legal guardian must execute documents and authorize decisions with respect to the account until the minor reaches the age of majority.
- ◆ The program will permit the account to be titled in the same way as any other account owned by the minor under the UTMA/UGMA. The custodian must notify the program administrator at the time the custodianship is terminated upon the child reaching legal age so that the account can be re-titled in the child's own name. The program generally prohibits a change in beneficiary, or any withdrawal that is not for the benefit of the minor, until the custodianship terminates.
- ◆ The program will title the account in the name of the adult acting as custodian but will provide a "check box" to indicate that the source of funds is an existing UTMA/UGMA account. The account will be restricted as to beneficiary changes and withdrawals until the custodianship terminates.

♦ The program will title the account in the name of the adult acting as custodian and will impose no special restrictions or requirements. The program administrator in this instance adopts the position that it is the custodian's legal responsibility to ensure that the account is handled in accordance within UTMA/UGMA laws.

5) Will the program accept a corporation or a trust as account owner?

A corporate-owned 529 account can provide unique benefits as part of a bonus plan or nonqualified deferred compensation plan. However, owners of closely-held corporations are often disappointed to learn that a 529 plan does not promise a tax-advantaged way to distribute corporate prof-its. Contributions made from company funds to an employee's or owner's 529 account are generally treated the same as cash payments made to the employee or owner.

The trustee of an irrevocable trust, attracted to the investment and tax advantages of a 529 plan, may decide to establish an account with a 529 plan and invest the trust's cash in the account, naming as 529 account beneficiary the beneficiary of the trust. Or, the individual owner of a 529 account may want to name a trust as successor owner, to make certain that in the event of the owner's death the account is used in accordance with his or her wishes. (Passing ownership directly to an individual successor owner could be viewed as too risky since control of those funds, including the power to take distributions, rests entirely with the new owner.)

Anyone planning to install a non-natural entity as owner or successor owner should seek professional advice from an attorney and an accoun-tant. Many legal and tax complications can arise in these situations.

6) Are interests in the 529 plan being sold through brokers?

If you rely on a financial advisor who earns commissions from the sale of investment products, chances are that the advisor will focus on 529 plans that pay a commission. This isn't necessarily bad. Most adviser-sold 529 plans are excellent programs and they often have the most flexible features. They have passed the scrutiny of your advisor's broker-dealer, and they provide a substantial amount of technical and administrative support to the financial advisor.

On the other hand, if you wish to conduct all the research and analysis on your own, or if you use a fee-only rather than commission-based financial planner, you will probably be more inclined to look for non-broker (i.e. direct-sold) 529 plans. You will generally incur lower expenses in direct-sold plans and your program selection will not be restricted to those that pay a commission.

With some advisor-sold 529 plans, a fee-based registered investment advisor (RIA) will have access to investments at net asset value, which means that the normal sales load is waived. The RIA will typically charge you a separate fee each quarter or year based on the amount of your assets he or she is managing.

Note that many direct-sold programs are prohibited by law from providing investment advice to you because they are not offered through licensed securities representatives or RIAs.

Several states restrict participation in their direct-sold 529 plans to residents, but make their advisor-sold 529 plans open to residents of any state.

7) What is the minimum contribution?

The issue here is your ability to make at least the minimum required contribution to the 529 plan. Some programs have no minimum contributions while others have minimum contributions as high as $250. Many savings programs waive the initial lump-sum minimum contribution if you commit to an automatic investment plan. In a prepaid program, the minimum contribution is the lowest-priced tuition package. But many prepaid programs also offer a monthly payment plan, albeit at a higher total cost.

8) Does the program accept contributions through payroll deduction and/or electronic funds transfer from your checking or savings account?

To contribute through payroll deduction or electronic funds transfer, make sure the program you select will accommodate it. Even if a program accepts contributions through payroll deduction, your employer must be able to meet the requirements of the program in establishing the payroll deduction process.

Many programs now permit online enrollment and contributions. This is a welcome convenience and can save time in establishing and funding a 529 account.

9) Does the 529 plan affiliate with a rewards program?

Upromise is a consumer-rewards program with a college savings tie-in. With this free service you earn rebates by making purchases from participating vendors, and you are given the option to have your rebates automatically deposited into an account at a 529 plan managed by Ascensus College Savings. A credit card available through Fidelity Investments, also offers cash-back rebates that can be automatically directed into one or more 529 plans. Participants in the Pennsylvania 529 plan are eligible for free scholarships at a number of private colleges through an arrangement with SAGE Scholars (www.sagescholars.com).

10) Does the program place any restrictions on your ownership rights or give any of these rights to the beneficiary?

Most 529 plans permit you as account owner to change the designated beneficiary, determine when and for what purpose distributions are made, and cancel the account and request a refund. But Michigan's prepaid tuition program, the Michigan Education Trust, is irrevocable and generally prohibits any refunds until after the beneficiary reaches age 18. Ownership rights affect several aspects of participation in a 529 plan, including financial-aid treatment, creditor actions, and eligibility for Medicaid, Social Security disability, food stamps and other similar programs.

11) Is an account in the program protected from the claims of creditors under state law?

A 529 plan offering special asset protection for participant accounts under state law may appeal to individuals with creditor concerns. Many states offer this protection, although the degree of protection may vary. If you are participating in a 529 plan outside your own state, discuss with an attorney how the asset protection provided by that state applies to creditor actions in your own state.

12) Can a non-owner make contributions to an account in the program?

To establish an account that other persons, including your relatives, can contribute to without opening their own accounts, the 529 plan must accommodate non-owner contributions. Nearly all now do. In fact, many plans have implemented online crowdfunding-like tools that make it easy for families to ask friends and loved ones to make a contribution. In most cases, the account owner sends a request via Facebook, Twitter or email, and gifts are received by a secure, electronic transfer.

New York was conspicuous in denying non-owner contributions in the past, but amended its laws in 2008 to permit them, although non-owner contributions are not eligible for the New York state-income tax deduction. Several unaffiliated websites—including CollegeBacker.com—also offer a friends-and-family registry service, while GiftofCollege.com offers 529 gift cards. Be sure to read and understand their rules, procedures, protections, and fees.

13) Does the program permit the account owner to designate a successor owner?

If you as account owner of a 529 plan were to die, your 529 account does not terminate. Instead, account ownership passes to a successor. Most programs make it easy for you to designate a successor owner at the time of enrollment, and permit you to submit a change in your designation at any time. If you do not designate a successor owner, the program will either automatically install a new owner at the time of your death, or pass ownership to your estate. If passed automatically, the chain of possible successors might start with the program beneficiary or your spouse, depending on the rules of the program.

14) How complete and accurate are the program disclosures?

The quality and quantity of program disclosures can vary among different 529 plans. Interests in a 529 savings program are "municipal fund securities" exempt from federal regulation; however, those distributed through broker-dealers must conform to the rules of the Municipal Securities Rulemaking Board, a self-regulatory organization responsible to the Securities and Exchange Commission. Some programs offer very extensive disclosures that answer most questions, while others are not quite so complete. All 529 savings programs have agreed to follow a set of disclosure principles first issued by the College Savings Plans Network in December 2004 and revised several times since then. Because of their structure, prepaid programs are not obligated to adopt those principles. With any 529 plan, check to see how current the program disclosures are and whether updated information is available on the official program website. You may also want to judge how knowledgeable and responsive the program call center is when you ask questions by telephone. If you are working with a financial advisor, be sure the advisor is willing and able to obtain education and technical support from the broker-dealer, program manager and/ or distributor.

15) How does the program report account activity to its participants?

Every 529 plan sends you a statement of your account at least annually, and many will send it more frequently. Perhaps you want online access to your account. Not all programs provide that. If you establish your account through a financial advisor, it may not appear along with other investments on your monthly or quarterly statements. However, the investment industry is making strides in capturing both 529 and non-529 investments for investors in one place through their record-keeping systems. You should also read and understand a program's privacy policy. This is usually not a concern and your account information should be exempt from any state "open document" laws (but ask if you are not sure).

Some programs will even print the unused contribution limit on monthly or quarterly account statements. (Most families will not be too concerned about this issue and will probably appreciate staying informed about the unused contribution limit.)

16) Has the IRS "qualified" the program?

A formal determination of qualified status from the IRS, although not required as a condition for a state to offer a 529 plan, can provide added comfort that the program is structured in compliance with Section 529 of the Code. Several programs applied for and received favorable determinations in the past. However, the IRS is no longer issuing such determinations[1] and states must rely on the legal opinions of their attorneys.

17) How does the program handle rollovers?

Although federal tax law permits you to roll over your account to another 529 plan without federal tax or penalty under certain conditions, not all 529 plans readily accommodate rollovers. Ideally, you will be able open an

---

1. IRS Rev. Proc. 2013-04, IRB 2013-01 (Jan. 2, 2013)

account with a new 529 plan and give authorization for a direct trustee-to-trustee rollover from your existing 529 account. The transfer is completed without your further involvement, and the Form 1099-Q you receive after the end of year will indicate that the transaction was a direct transfer between plans. Some savings programs charge a small fee on an outbound rollover. You must still comply with the requirements for qualified roll-overs in order for it to be tax free (see chapter 3).

If the 529 plan you wish to roll into does not agree to initiate and coordinate a direct trustee-to-trustee rollover, or your existing plan refuses to send the money directly to a new plan, you can still accomplish the rollover, but you will have to take a distribution and within 60 days re-contribute the funds to a new 529 plan.

In prepaid programs, your decision to transfer your investment to another 529 plan (savings or prepaid) may require a full or partial cancellation of your contract, and the financial consequences may be more significant. Be sure to investigate this before signing up with a prepaid program. If you wish to roll over an existing 529 account to a prepaid program, you will need to find out if the prepaid program accepts rollover contributions. For example, Florida's prepaid program does not.

Section 2: Investment and expense characteristics

The second section of this checklist involves an evaluation of the investment and expense characteristics of the program to determine which programs best meet your college savings objectives.

18) Does the program offer a college-savings strategy consistent with your own objectives and preferences?

This is the essential issue for most investors. What do I get for the money I contribute? How will my investment perform? How much risk am I accepting? How does it compare to other 529 plans, and to other types of investments? You will need to carefully consider what happens to your money after it is contributed to the program, and make the decision to join only after you become comfortable with its investment approach.

19) Does the 529 plan provide a "guarantee" that your investment will keep up with the increasing costs of college?

A "yes" answer is the hallmark of a 529 prepaid program or guaranteed savings program, while a "no" answer indicates a 529 savings program. A savings program will not promise that your account will keep pace with any measure of increasing college costs (with very limited exceptions, such as Alaska's program that offers an option guaranteeing a minimum return equivalent to tuition increases at the University of Alaska, but only for beneficiaries who end up attending the University of Alaska). You have the potential to do better than the college cost inflation rate, but you also have the risk of seeing your account lag behind college costs.

20) Does the 529 savings program offer an "age-based" asset allocation strategy, a menu of "static" portfolios, or both?

An age-based or matriculation-based strategy is one in which your account is automatically moved to a more conservative asset allocation over time. Typically, the age of your beneficiary will determine the portfolio in the program into which your contributions are initially placed, although it is now common that a program will base the initial portfolio on the expected number of years to matriculation rather than age, or will simply allow you to choose your starting point from any of the program's age-based portfolios.

The idea of an age-based asset allocation strategy is that you will want to be more aggressively invested when your investment time horizon is long (e.g. for a young child's college savings), and so your account will be invested primarily in stock funds. Over time, your account will gradually be shifted out of stock funds and into fixed-income and/or money market funds. It finally comes to rest in the most conservative age-based portfolio until fully withdrawn.

Savings programs manipulate their age-based asset allocations through one of the following two mechanisms. The first is by establishing a series of portfolios where each portfolio has a target asset allocation among stock, bond, and money market funds that generally does not change over time. Your account is transferred ("migrated") from one portfolio to the next at scheduled intervals. The second approach is to assign your account to a portfolio targeted to a particular year of use. Instead of moving your account from one portfolio to the next, the manager adjusts the underlying investments of the portfolio to achieve new asset allocation targets over time. Only when the target year of use is reached is the account transferred to a final "resting" portfolio.

Is one approach better than the other? Not necessarily. The first, in which your account is transferred among increasingly conservative portfolios, is more mechanical yet more disciplined. You will know "going in" how your account is to be allocated among stocks, bonds, and money market funds at any point in the future. The second approach is less mechanical and gives the portfolio investment manager a greater amount of discretion in adjusting the asset allocation for changing market conditions.

A "static" option in a savings program is one in which your portfolio's targeted asset allocation does not change over time. It can be a 100% equity option, a 100% fixed-income option, or a pre-determined blend of different asset classes. Many of the static options are assembled as "funds of funds," combining two or more underlying mutual funds within a given portfolio. These portfolios are often labeled the "asset allocation" options. An increasing number of programs now offer individual-fund portfolios in addition to multi-fund and other options.

21) Does the program offer a principal-protected option?

If you have no tolerance for downside risk with your investments, consider a savings program with an interest-bearing investment option that protects the value of your principal. There are several different types of principal-protected options found among 529 plans. Be aware that the amount of interest you earn may not keep pace with increasing college costs.

Many 529 plans offer a money market option. A money market fund consists of short-term securities and is designed to maintain a level unit price, although its dividend/interest payout can swing dramatically over a short period of time.

Some programs (including most of the programs managed by TIAA-CREF) offer "guaranteed" options that not only protect principal but guarantee a minimum level of interest. The actual rate is declared on an annual or quarterly basis and can be higher than the minimum rate. The investment is typically backed by a "funding agreement" with a life insurance company. Another variation found in the 529 marketplace is the "stable value" investment. This is a product that seeks to combine the stable share pricing of a money market fund with the higher returns of a bond fund. By leveling the yields of its underlying fixed-income securities, it also produces less variability in overall yield.

Over twenty plans are now offering FDIC-insured bank products in their 529 savings programs, including certificates of deposit and bank savings accounts.

22) What are the other characteristics of the underlying securities in the options available under a savings program?

This book does not purport to provide a technical analysis of investments. However, you should attempt to determine the investment fundamentals of portfolios in a 529 plan (or rely on a professional who can) and see that it fits well with your other investments (retirement accounts, etc.). Ask the following questions:

- How is the portfolio allocated among stocks, bonds, and money market funds?
- How much of the portfolio is invested in international stocks, junk bonds, large-cap, medium-cap, and small-cap stocks?

- Who manages the underlying mutual funds?
- What are the track records of those funds?
- Does the program require that you develop your own "portfolio" by allocating your contributions among individual mutual funds (or permit you to do so)?

Some 529 savings programs invest in mutual funds from one particular fund family (typically an affiliate of the 529 program manager), while others are "multi-manager," incorporating funds from two or more separate fund families. Under either model, the investment history of most 529 plans has not been long enough to make conclusive comparisons, although a detailed analysis of various portfolios can yield useful information. Many 529 plans now post 529 portfolio performance on their websites with the information updated either daily, monthly, or quarterly.

23) Does the program permit contributions to be allocated among multiple options?

If the answer is "no," you will have to open separate accounts for the same beneficiary if you wish to use more than one investment option. In plans that charge an account management fee, multiple accounts may mean multiple fees (see #27 below).

24) How quickly does the program invest your contribution?

Not all 529 plans possess the administrative capabilities to ensure that your contribution is invested within a day or two of when your check is received. This can be of particular concern at certain times during the year, most notably late December when a large inflow of contributions can overwhelm processing capacities. The day on which your contribution is processed can also depend on the method you use in making your contribution. For example, it may take longer to process an initial contribution using an electronic funds transfer from your bank account than one made by check.

A delay means that you will not have the benefit (or possible detriment) of market activity during that time. A program that is not managed by an outside investment firm may lack the administrative resources needed to process investments on a daily basis. For example, in the Virginia529 inVEST plan, the investment of your contribution can take several days (the "pending settlement period").

25) How are earnings in the portfolio credited to your account?

The vast majority of savings programs use daily valuation. You own "shares" of the program trust fund and the price of those shares will reflect the daily share prices of the underlying funds, along with any investment earnings and program expenses posted to the trust fund. A small number of programs use balance-forward accounting for one or more of their investment options, where earnings are posted to individual accounts on a regular basis, but not updated daily.

26) Does the program charge an enrollment fee or sales charge?

Some 529 plans charge a small enrollment fee and others do not. Sometimes the enrollment fee is waived, or the amount reduced, in particular circumstances (e.g., for state residents or during special promotions). If you open multiple accounts for the same beneficiary, or for beneficiaries in the same family, the program may offer a discount off normal enrollment fees. Because it is a fixed charge, the effect of any enrollment fee on your overall return will depend on how much money you invest in the program.

If you are enrolling in a 529 plan through a financial advisor receiving commissions, there may be a sales charge or "load" depending on which "class" of shares or units you choose to purchase. The upfront load on an "A" unit may be as little as 1% or as much as 5.75% of your contribution. "B" units typically do not involve an upfront load, but incur a "deferred" sales charge if you liquidate your investment within a certain period of time. For example, a B unit may be subject to a 5% deferred sales charge if liquidated anytime during the first year, declining in steps to 1% in year five before it drops to zero. "C" units generally are not subject to an upfront sales charge, but are often subject to a 1% deferred sales charge for the first 12 months after purchase. The price you pay for a lower C-unit sales charge structure is higher ongoing annual expense compared to A units.

Broker-dealers have a fiduciary responsibility to select the most appropriate share class for their client based on their investment time horizon. Generally, A-shares are recommended when the beneficiary is less than 10 years old, and C-shares are recommended when the beneficiary is older than 10. In recent years, the Financial Industry Regulatory Authority Inc. (FINRA) has stepped up scrutiny of 529 plans, making sure proper due diligence has been performed when choosing a share class. Some 529 plans have responded by launching shares that transition automatically into a lower-cost share class after a set period of time (typically C-shares that convert to A-shares). Convertible shares help ensure the 529 plan account owner pays the lowest available fees over the life of their investment, and we expect more plans to follow this trend in the future.

For investors with substantial sums to invest through a commission-based advisor, "breakpoint" pricing is often available for A units. The upfront sales load is reduced or eliminated for account balances above certain breakpoints or for purchase commitments above those breakpoints. Some 529 plans will include the mutual funds you have in taxable accounts or IRAs with the same fund family that manages the 529 plan when determining your eligibility for breakpoints, while other 529 plans will not aggregate those accounts. If you are looking to invest substantial sums in a 529 plan, be sure to investigate your eligibility for breakpoint pricing.

27) Does the program charge an annual account maintenance fee?

An account maintenance fee is a fixed-dollar amount charged against your account on a quarterly, semi-annual, or annual basis. These fees can vary from $10 to $50 per year. In some programs, the account maintenance fee is waived if you have a specified account balance or commit to an automatic investment plan.

28) What is the program's annualized expense ratio?

The expense ratio of a savings program typically consists of two components. The first is the total of any asset-based fees charged against the value of the program fund by the outside program manager and/or state agency in charge of administering the 529 plan. The second consists of the expenses of the underlying mutual funds, which can range from very low-cost index funds to relatively high-cost international equity or other specialized sector funds. In some savings programs there is a third source of expense—certain administrative costs charged to the program fund, such as the cost of an annual audit—although these expenses tend to have a relatively small impact.

Some program managers include, or "wrap," the underlying mutual fund expenses in the management fees they charge to the 529 plan, resulting in one "all in" expense ratio that remains constant over time. The advantage to this approach is that it presents a simple and easy-to-understand fee structure, and there is no incentive for the program manager to select mutual funds with high underlying fees. A possible disadvantage is that the investor with a conservative asset allocation may be paying the same expense as the investor with an aggressive asset allocation, despite the fact that bond and money market funds generally have lower expense ratios than stock funds.

Total asset-based expenses in direct-sold 529 savings programs currently range from 0.00% annually to over 1%. Programs distributed through commissioned-based advisors will charge additional annual asset-based fees used to compensate the advisor. An example of this would be a program that charges an extra 0.25% annual fee for A units (along with an upfront sales load discussed above) or an extra 0.60% annual fee for C units that do not convert. Actual expenses vary among programs.

Considering the valuable tax benefits available with a 529 plan, and the special effort required to design, market, and administer a plan, the total fixed-dollar and asset-based expenses associated with most programs are very reasonable. But with the wide range and variety of expenses, and the significant impact they can have on your overall investment return, you should place special emphasis on expenses when choosing a 529 plan.

29) Are there charges for other transactions?

Some programs may impose a charge on beneficiary changes, account owner changes, rollovers, and certain other requests.

30) Can you claim a state income tax deduction for any or all of your contributions to the program?

Thirty-four states and the District of Columbia offer a state income tax deduction or credit for contributions to 529 plans. Most require that you use the in-state 529 plan to be eligible for the tax benefit, and depending on your state income tax bracket and any limits placed on the amount of your deduction, this can be a powerful incentive for choosing your own state's program. Arizona, Arkansas, Kansas, Minnesota, Missouri, Montana and Pennsylvania allow a deduction for contributions to any 529 plan, not just the home-state plan. Any of these seven states may ultimately reverse course and restrict deductions to their in-state programs. Some other states, however, may eventually decide to extend their deductions to contributions made to out-of-state 529 plans.

Be sure you understand how the tax deduction in your state, if any, is structured. Here are some important questions:

- If the contributor is not the same as the account owner, which person claims the deduction?
- Is there a cap on the amount of deduction that can be claimed each year? If so, is the maximum deduction computed per contributor, per tax return, per beneficiary, or per account?

♦ Can contributions in excess of any annual deduction limit be carried over to future tax years?
♦ Does the account beneficiary have to be related in any particular way to the contributor? Can you claim a deduction for an account you establish for yourself?

If your state offers a state income tax deduction, you should recognize the circumstances under which you may be required to "recapture" the tax deduction in a future year. Most states require that you recapture prior deductions if you take a nonqualified distribution, and some states will apply the recapture to outbound rollovers as well. If you can claim a deduction for only a portion of your contributions, you will need to understand the ordering rules for recapture if only a portion of your account is withdrawn for non-qualified purposes. You may find, however, that your state has not yet fully explained how recapture applies in all situations. If you are taking a distribution to pay for K-12 tuition expenses, be sure to check with your plan to make sure it will be considered qualified. At the time of this publication, not all states have conformed with the federal law to include K-12 tuition as a qualified expense.

> **You can calculate the value of your state tax deduction by visiting Savingforcollege.com/statetax**

31) Does the program offer any other financial incentives?

Providing a state income tax break is not the only way a state can encourage participation in 529 plans. Several states offer a partial match for contributions made by low-income and moderate-income residents into their 529 savings programs. New Jersey provides a first-year scholarship of as much as $1,500 to New Jersey beneficiaries attending a New Jersey public or private university. Louisiana provides an earnings enhancement equal to 2% to 14% (depending on income) of contributions. A number of states will disregard balances in their own 529 plans when determining student eligibility for state-funded financial aid programs.

These are all examples of how states are striving to make their programs as attractive as possible.

32) What is the term of the program manager?

The fact that a particular financial services firm has been selected to manage a 529 plan does not mean that the program will be using that manager forever. Management contracts are subject to terms of anywhere from two to 30 years. At the end of the initial program term, the contract may be extended or, if the contract is re-bid, the manager may be replaced. Naturally, in the event the manager is replaced, the program will probably look much different under the new manager.

Besides manager changes, many other aspects of a program are subject to change at any time. Thus far, most changes we have witnessed have benefited participants, but there is no guarantee that it will always be that way.

33) How popular is the program?

As a general rule, you want to join a 529 plan that has proven to be popular with other investors, or at least one that has the prospect of becoming popular. Level of assets in the program can be an indicator of popularity, although you need to consider several factors: how long the program has been around in its current form; restrictions on participation such as state residency, age, etc.; population of the sponsoring state; and whether the program is being distributed on a nationwide basis through financial advisors.

Programs must attract a sufficient level of assets in order to generate the revenues needed to pay for administration, investment management, and oversight. If the program is unable to achieve critical size, it becomes more likely that changes will be made, and these changes can be dramatic. While a replacement or addition of a program manager or changes to the investment offerings can be positive, other alterations, such as an increase in fees and expenses to cover the costs of operation, can be negative. The worst result is where the state, or the firm hired as program manager, loses its enthusiasm for the program and scales back its resources or the amount of attention it devotes.

Although it is impossible to establish a strict standard, any program at least three years old that has not yet attracted $150 million in assets can be considered small. A large 529 plan would be one with over $1 billion in assets. The largest prepaid program in the country is Florida's with over $11 billion in assets. The largest savings program currently is Virginia's CollegeAmerica, managed by American Funds, with over $61 billion at the end of 2017.

Another way to gauge program popularity is to search for articles in the local and regional press. Often, the media are able to pick up on developments or concerns by keeping tabs with state and program officials. Occasionally, a state's 529 plan becomes fodder in the political wrangling that characterizes many state legislatures and official offices.

34) Does the program rely on a state subsidy?

Most states expect their 529 programs to generate revenues sufficient to cover operating costs. A few states still find it necessary to subsidize program operations. A state subsidy to the program can help keep costs low for the participant, but budget cuts in the future may cause an increase in the fees charged to your account. Louisiana is a good example of a state that keeps fees low by paying the administrative costs for its 529 savings program out of state coffers.

Section 3: Avoidable restrictions

This third section describes restrictions or hazards that may be evident in a program but can be avoided through a timely rollover to another 529 plan without those problems. The ability to roll over your account means an unacceptable provision in any particular program should not necessarily eliminate it from contention. You simply have to recognize the appropriate time to make the rollover, and any costs associated with the rollover. Watch out especially for the contingent deferred sales charges in advisor-sold 529 plans. These charges, typically associated with the purchase of B or C units, are avoided only by keeping your money in the 529 plan for a specified number of years.

35) Are there any penalties or fees for withdrawing your money from the program?

Some programs may charge a fixed dollar fee (e.g., $50) on a nonqualified distribution which can be avoided by first rolling over to another 529 plan.

36) Are distributions from the program exempt from your state's income tax?

For most people, qualified distributions from any 529 plan are exempt from their state income taxes, and they don't have to worry about this issue when choosing a 529 plan. Alabama is the lone exception; qualified distributions from an Alabama 529 plan are exempt from Alabama tax, but qualified distributions from a non-Alabama plan are not. Legislation has been introduced in the Alabama legislature to "fix" this problem, but it had not passed by the time this book went to press. An Alabama resident using an out-of-state 529 plan may wish to roll over to the Alabama 529 plan before taking distributions to pay for college.

Also consider that you may be living in a state that exempts a distribution attributable to the beneficiary's death, disability, or receipt of a scholarship, but only when the distribution is from the in-state 529 plan. (Such distributions are taxable nonqualified distributions for federal tax purposes, although the 10 percent penalty is waived.) Under certain circumstances, you may wish to rollover from an out-of-state 529 plan to your in-state 529 plan to take advantage of this particular exemption.

37) Are there any time or age limits on the use of the account?

If the 529 plan requires that the account be used within a certain number of years, for example, simply roll over the account to another state's program prior to reaching that point.

38) Is there a minimum time period before taking qualified or nonqualified distributions from your account?

While a few states in the past placed a several-month, or several-year, minimum holding period on contributions made to their 529 savings plans, nearly all of these restrictions have since been removed. All 529 savings programs will, however, deny or delay distribution requests made within the first several days after receiving a contribution to be certain that your check clears. Because of the different manner in which 529 prepaid programs operate, many of them will require that your account be open for a certain number of years before you can receive full benefits.

39) Are there other withdrawal restrictions that can be avoided by rolling over to another 529 plan?

Here are some examples:

- ◆ Your program has cumbersome substantiation requirements of education expenses that other 529 plans may not have.
- ◆ Your program requires that the account owner be treated as the recipient of any undocumented distributions while other 529 plans give you the option of directing the distribution to your beneficiary (thereby shifting the income to a lower tax bracket).
- ◆ Your program will only pay a qualified distribution directly to the beneficiary's school, and does not give you the option of having the qualified distribution made payable to the beneficiary.

♦ Your program has a minimum distribution amount or limit on frequency of distributions that other programs do not have.

40) Will the program approve a request to transfer ownership of the account?

There are a number of reasons why you may decide you want to transfer ownership of your 529 account to someone else. One possibility is that an account you own may be subject to the claims of your creditors. Another possibility is that you do not want your account considered a countable asset for Medicaid purposes. Finally, you may at some point decide that you just do not want to be responsible for the management of the 529 account and would like someone else to handle it. The last two possibilities are particularly relevant for grandparents.

Some 529 plans do not approve requests for a transfer of ownership prior to your death or incapacity, or a court order in a divorce or other legal proceeding. To accomplish such a change, you would have to first roll over your account to another 529 plan that does permit owner transfers.

41) How much can be contributed to an account in the program?

One of the requirements for qualification under Section 529 is that the program establishes procedures so that participants do not contribute more than needed for the beneficiary's future qualified higher education expenses. These maximum contribution limits can vary significantly among 529 plans, with some savings programs below $300,000 per beneficiary and others in excess of $450,000.

If you plan on making very large contributions, you should be sure to understand how the limit is applied. In general, the maximum contribution limit refers to the account balance which, when reached, requires the program administrator to reject further contributions. In some plans, but not typically, the account balance limit is reduced once you begin taking qualified distributions. In no case will your account be prevented from growing in value beyond the stated limit.

Many 529 plans will increase their contribution account-balance limits periodically as the cost of college attendance rises. But what do you do if the 529 plan you are interested in does not permit you to contribute as much as you think you should invest for your beneficiary's future higher education costs? The answer would be to open accounts in more than one program. Although all accounts in the same state with the same beneficiary must be aggregated, the IRS does not require that a 529 plan consider balances in other states' programs when applying its limits. Although this may seem like an easy way to get around the individual state limits, exercise caution. You are looking for trouble if you open accounts in multiple programs simply as a way to shelter more assets than you can reasonably anticipate as the amount your beneficiary will need for college and graduate school. A state that determines that you are intentionally exceeding your investment need for higher education costs can terminate your account and possibly charge extra penalties. You may also subject yourself to extra scrutiny from the IRS.

SEVEN

Income Tax Planning with 529 Plans

The three major income tax benefits associated with 529 plans—tax-deferred growth, the tax exclusion for earnings withdrawn for qualified purposes, and the possible shifting of earnings to a low-income tax bracket when withdrawn for non-qualified purposes—are explained in detail in chapter 3. Once the basic federal rules are understood, the next step is to explore income tax planning opportunities associated with 529 plans. This chapter will help you do that. Below is a discussion of several income-tax planning considerations related to 529 plans.

In which years should I take distributions from my 529 account?

Naturally, you should take distributions in years when the earnings are excluded and avoid taking distributions that generate taxable income and incur the 10 percent penalty tax. This is not as easy as it sounds. A lot will depend on when the beneficiary is attending college; which years, if any, you choose to take withdrawals for K-12 tuition expenses; the expenses that will be incurred; the amount of money in your 529 account; the amount of untaxed earnings in the account; your tax brackets; and the other tax benefits that may be available to you and your beneficiary. Fitting all the pieces together in one plan for an optimal tax result can be challenging. Be sure to consider the following:

1) American Opportunity and Lifetime Learning credits

Avoid using your 529 account to pay for 100 percent of qualifying college costs in a year when you or your beneficiary will be claiming one of these credits. Otherwise, as explained in chapter 3, claiming the credit will cause some portion of your 529 distribution to be subject to income tax. Instead, consider using other non–529 resources to pay for some of the expenses and spreading your 529 distributions between years to effectively capture qualified expenses above the amount of expenses that are applied to the credit. It is important to realize that the type of credit you claim can make a significant difference. The American Opportunity credit "consumes" up to $4,000 of tuition and related expenses while the Lifetime Learning credit consumes up to $10,000 of these expenses.

> *Example:* Steve has a 529 account worth $40,000 for his daughter Amy. It consists of $30,000 basis and $10,000 earnings. Amy incurs qualified higher education expenses totaling $25,000 each year for four years. Assuming no further growth in the account, Steve withdraws $25,000 from his 529 account in Year 1 and the remaining $15,000 in Year 2 to pay those expenses. However, because either Steve or Amy claims the maximum $2,500 American Opportunity credit, Amy's qualified higher education expenses for 529 purposes is reduced in each of those four years by the $4,000 used to generate the credit. The $25,000 in distributions for Year 1 now consists of $21,000 in qualified distributions and $4,000 in nonqualified distributions. (The $15,000 in distributions during Year 2 remain entirely tax-free because Amy has $21,000 in qualified expenses even after the $4,000 reduction for

tax-credit expenses.) The recipient of the distributions (either Steve or Amy) has to report $1,000 in income for Year 1, calculated by multiplying the account's 25% earnings ratio times the $4,000 in nonqualified distributions.

To avoid this result, Steve could have limited his 529 account distributions to $21,000 for Year 1 expenses, and used $4,000 from an education loan or other non–529 source. He would then have had an extra $4,000 to withdraw from his 529 account for Year 2 expenses. But Steve failed to talk to his accountant in time. Fortunately, the 10 percent penalty tax is waived to the extent a nonqualified distribution is caused by the tax credit adjustment. Furthermore, by making Amy or her college the recipient of the distributions, the earnings will be reported on Amy's tax return and she may be in a lower tax bracket than Steve.

2) Financial aid eligibility

Chapter 4 explains how parent and student income from the base year (the year prior to filing the FAFSA aid application) will cause an increase in the student's expected family contribution (EFC) and a decrease in need-based financial aid. Any action that results in reportable income—e.g. a nonqualified distribution from a 529 plan, or a capital gain from the sale of mutual funds—should be delayed to the calendar year in which the student enters their junior year of college (assuming they will graduate in four years).

How will use of a 529 plan affect my state income taxes?

State tax planning can be important in getting the most tax benefits from a 529 plan. Many states provide an income tax deduction for all or a portion of your contributions to a 529 plan. Most of these states require that you use the in-state 529 plan to earn the deduction, but a small number of states have laws that permit the deduction for contributions to any state's 529 plan. Be sure you understand the rules in the state where you live.

If state deductions are available but are subject to a maximum annual amount, consider spreading out your contributions over two or more years rather than contributing one amount higher than the deduction limit. This won't be necessary in a state that allows you to carry forward your excess contributions to future tax years.

Most states allowing a deduction for contributions will require recapture of those deductions if nonqualified distributions are taken in later years. This recapture will be in addition to the earnings portion of the nonqualified distribution reportable on the state return. Be sure to understand how the recapture rules work for the 529 plan in your state. For example, some states may require that a pro-rata amount of your deduction be recaptured anytime a nonqualified distribution is taken, while others will recapture your deduction only after total nonqualified distributions exceed your non-deductible contributions into the 529 plan.

Are there any tax benefits in opening multiple accounts for my child?

Establishing multiple 529 accounts in different 529 plans can provide you with an opportunity to better control the amount and timing of distributed earnings. Each 529 account will have a different earnings ratio depending on its investment history, making it possible to take withdrawals on a selective basis. This strategy is similar to selecting certain mutual fund shares to sell based on their unrealized gains or losses. A 529 savings account established ten years prior to college is probably going to have a higher earnings ratio than an account established one year prior to college.

It may also be possible to achieve this positioning by placing different types of investments into different accounts. For example, if you seek to diversify your college savings with a 50/50 blend of stocks and bonds, consider opening one 529 account with a 100% stock portfolio and a second account in a different 529 plan with a 100% bond portfolio. Your two accounts will develop different earnings ratios as determined by their respective investment performance.

In years with sufficient qualified expenses, you would normally decide to withdraw from the account with the highest earnings ratio because the earnings will be excluded from taxable income. Withdrawals from the account with the lowest earnings ratio should be targeted for any years in which you decide to take a nonqualified distribution.

Of course, if all distributions are being used to pay for college and tax-free anyway, there is no strategic value in maintaining separate accounts. It is only when there is a nonqualified distribution producing taxable income that this can become useful.

In a down market, the isolation of asset classes in separate accounts may produce the opportunity to claim a tax loss that might not exist with a single balanced account. You could liquidate the account showing a net loss while retaining the account showing a net gain. Chapter 12 explains how 529 losses may be deducted under certain conditions on your income tax return.

Should I borrow money to invest in a 529 plan?

It could make sense to fund a college savings account with borrowed money. The interest paid on the debt may produce an income tax deduction for you at a high tax bracket, while the 529 earnings may escape taxation altogether.

The tax law contains a prohibition against deducting interest on debt used to produce tax-exempt income. If you borrow money to invest in tax-free municipal bonds, for example, the interest expense on the loan is not deductible.[1] A critical question is whether the exclusion of qualified 529 distributions invokes the prohibition against deducting interest on borrowings. The answer appears to be "no," simply because the distributions are not, per-se, exempt. Unless certain hurdles are cleared the distributed earnings become taxable. However, some caution is warranted as the IRS has not yet ruled on this specific issue.

Another question to be explored in considering whether to borrow is the character of the interest expense on the loan. If the interest were

---

1. Code Section 265(a)(2)

considered investment interest expense, it would be deductible as an itemized deduction. (But only to the extent you have investment income. Any excess investment interest expense is carried forward indefinitely and deducted against investment income in future years.)

It is doubtful, however, that the interest on debt used to fund a 529 contribution is investment interest, despite the fact that the debt proceeds are being deposited into an investment account with the 529 plan. The IRS can take a position that the debt was incurred for personal purposes, and not for investment purposes, because the contribution into the 529 plan is treated as a gift, and gifts are personal in nature. If this is correct, the interest on the debt is classified as nondeductible personal interest.

In order to avoid the characterization problem, the best way to borrow for 529 funding purposes is with a home equity loan. Interest on qualifying home-equity indebtedness of up to $100,000 is deductible on Schedule A of Form 1040, no matter what use is made of the borrowed funds. The home equity loan must be on a first or second home. The interest on home-equity indebtedness used for this purpose is not deductible for purposes of the alternative minimum tax (AMT), so be careful in determining whether you are subject to the AMT.

Once you are comfortable that your home-equity loan interest can be deducted, calculate the after-tax interest rate on your loan. A taxpayer in a 30% combined tax bracket with a 4% interest loan is paying 2.8% interest after-tax (70% times 4%). The after-tax interest rate can then be compared to the expected return of your 529 account—assuming you can count on distributions being tax-free. An investment return above 2.8% in the above example means the investor is coming out ahead.

Of course, there may be many other things to think about before borrowing for this purpose. Cash flow impact is one. The loan will need to be paid back over time, while your investment presumably stays in the 529 plan until the college years. Impact on your borrowing ability for other purposes could be another consideration. And finally, there is the risk that the college savings account may not perform as well as originally anticipated, and the leveraging strategy could lose money.

What can I do if the beneficiary of my 529 account graduates from college and I still have money left in the account?

You can either withdraw the money, with the earnings portion of any withdrawal subject to federal income tax and the 10 percent penalty, or you can leave it in the account to continue growing tax-deferred. If you leave it in, you can keep the same beneficiary on the account (despite having graduated) or you can change the beneficiary to a qualifying family member.

Let's say that you no longer want to maintain the 529 account and would like the excess funds distributed. If the account beneficiary is in a lower tax bracket, you may want to request that the distribution be made to the beneficiary so that the earnings are reported in the beneficiary's name and social security number. However, you need to be careful with this strategy. If your child is subject to the kiddie tax, you will not be able to take advantage of the lower tax brackets. The kiddie tax can apply to children as old as 23 (see chapter 11).

Regardless of the recipient of a nonqualified distribution, the 10 percent federal penalty will be owed on the earnings portion of the distribution unless it is eligible for one of the penalty exceptions explained in chapter 3.

Does a 529 account have to be for college?

The obvious attraction of tax-deferred earnings may cause some investors to consider putting money into a 529 savings plan account without actually intending to use the account to pay for higher education expenses. After all, if the account is later withdrawn, the added penalty is only 10 percent applied against the earnings portion of the distribution, and a few financial calculations may suggest that the tax deferral benefits can overcome the penalty after a sufficient number of years.

Naturally, this strategy would be viewed by many as an abuse of the tax laws. Although Section 529 does not contain any explicit language that would put the individual investor at risk, the statute does assign some responsibility to the state by defining a 529 savings plan as one "under which a person may make contributions to an account which is established for the purpose of meeting the qualified higher education expenses of the designated beneficiary of the account." If investors establish accounts for a different purpose—namely the deferral of income—the tax-qualified status of the program may be in jeopardy. Some states, but certainly not all, have developed program rules that permit the program administrator to reject contributions or terminate accounts if it is determined that the account was established for a purpose other than the payment of the named beneficiary's qualified higher education expenses. The Pension Protection Act of 2006 also gives the Treasury Department additional authority to issue anti-abuse regulations in the future.

It can be argued that concerns about abuse are overblown. Many individuals are returning to school at a later age, even after retirement, and funding a 529 plan for that purpose is entirely appropriate. Even those who now have only a vague interest in returning to school may later decide to act on it once they have funds tucked away in a 529 plan account. There is also the option to pass down a 529 plan balance to a future generation, to help pay for a grandchild's private K-12 or college education. Furthermore, the strategy of "overfunding" a 529 account for reasons of tax deferral can easily backfire. In a political environment that rewards taxable investors with low tax rates on capital gains and certain other types of investment income, the risk of having highly-taxed income and penalties on a future nonqualified 529 distribution is sufficient to cause the overwhelming majority of investors to limit their 529 contributions to truly-anticipated future college costs.

EIGHT

Estate Planning with 529 Plans

The estate and gift tax rules surrounding 529 plans are unique and the planning considerations are anything but straightforward. In fact, the gift tax provisions contained in Section 529 fly in the face of the general gift tax rules contained elsewhere in the Internal Revenue Code.

The law provides that a contribution into a 529 plan after August 5, 1997 is treated as a completed gift from the donor to the account's designated beneficiary. Further, the gift is considered a gift of a "present interest" that qualifies for the $15,000 gift tax annual exclusion, despite the fact that in nearly all 529 plans the designated beneficiary never has rights to the money.[1] The portion of the contribution covered by the $15,000 exclusion is also excluded for purposes of the generation-skipping transfer tax.

Section 529 goes one step further and provides an election that allows the donor to treat a contribution of more than the annual exclusion amount as occurring ratably over five years for gift tax purposes. This means you can contribute as much as $75,000 in 2015 to the account of

---

1. The annual gift exclusion amount is adjusted for cost of living increases, in increments of $1,000. In 2018, the exclusion amount is $15,000.

one designated beneficiary without creating a taxable gift, assuming you make no other gifts to that beneficiary during the five-year period 2018–2022. Although not contained in the statute, the IRS takes the position that if a contribution of more than $75,000 is made to a 529 plan, the averaging election applies only to the first $50,000 and the remainder is treated as a gift in the year of contribution. The five-year election is made on the federal gift tax return, Form 709.

The value of the 529 account is excluded from your gross estate, with one possible exception. If you make the five-year election but then die before the first day of the fifth calendar year, the portion of the contribution allocated to calendar years beginning after your death is included in your estate.

> **Visit Savingforcollege.com/superfund to see how much more you can save with the 5-year election**

Besides the five-year election, what is so unique about these rules?

The most startling aspect of the Section 529 gift and estate rules is that you can continue to exercise nearly complete control over your account. The account owner can change the designated beneficiary to another qualifying family member at will. Further, you will have the option to simply terminate the account and receive a refund of the account value, subject to income tax and a federal 10 percent additional tax on the earnings. While this rescission may defeat the purpose of removing value from an estate, it certainly provides the level of control and flexibility that many individuals seek when talking to advisors about gifting and other estate-reduction strategies.

If you change the designated beneficiary to a qualified family member, no further gift is involved, unless the new beneficiary belongs to a lower generation than the former beneficiary.[2] If the new designation crosses the generation boundary, the former beneficiary is treated as making a gift to the new beneficiary subject to all the normal gift tax rules. In this situation, the special five-year election can be made by the former beneficiary, if necessary, to minimize or avoid gift tax consequences.

Under usual estate and gift tax principles, the level of control enjoyed by the account owner would most assuredly cause the contribution to be treated as an incomplete gift and the value of the account to remain in his or her gross estate. In fact, this was precisely the treatment accorded contributions to a 529 plan from the time Section 529 was signed into law on August 20, 1996 until August 5, 1997, when it was amended by the Taxpayer Relief Act of 1997. A contribution made to a 529 plan during that one-year span was not treated as a gift. The subsequent withdrawal to pay for educational expenses was not treated as a gift either, because it was deemed to be a direct payment of tuition, and direct payments of tuition (and medical care) on behalf of another individual are not counted as gifts.[3]

How much can I remove from my estate by using a 529 plan?

Most 529 savings programs accept contributions of $300,000 or more for each child, grandchild, or other beneficiary. Contributions of this magnitude are sure to exceed the gift tax annual exclusion, even with the five-year election, and the excess will be a taxable gift. Your $11.18 million (in 2018) lifetime exemption for gifts can be employed to shelter such large contributions. To the extent you dip into your lifetime exemption for gifts, the amount of exemption for your estate (also $11.18 million) is reduced. Grandparents making substantial contributions for grandchildren must also consider the generation-skipping transfer (GST) tax. The GST exemption follows the same schedule as the estate tax exemption.

---

2. The rules for determining the assignment of generation to any particular individual are contained in Code Section 2651.

3. Code Section 2503(e) describes the exclusion for certain transfers of educational and medical expenses.

Many contributors to 529 plans will attempt to stay within the bounds of the annual exclusion. This can still add up to a substantial sum, especially with the five-year election. Consider the wealthy couple with four children. With each parent contributing $75,000 to the 529 plan account of each child in 2018, this couple can effectively remove $600,000 from their combined estates in one day without using up a single dollar of their lifetime exemptions. Not only is the value of their 529 accounts removed from their taxable estates, they are invested in portfolios that can appreciate over time without the drag of income taxes. And so the estate tax savings will grow even more substantially. That's effective estate planning!

Why should I contribute to a 529 plan when I can make direct tuition payments to reduce my estate?

A grandparent may be planning to make use of the unlimited gift tax exclusion under Code Section 2503(e) for the direct payment of tuition to an educational institution. To the extent that tuition is paid with non–529 assets, the funds in a 529 plan may not be needed for college. Note, however, that the exclusion for direct payment of education expenses applies only to tuition, while a 529 plan may allow funding for all qualified higher education expenses.

There are other reasons to consider funding a 529 plan now even if you intend to make direct payments of tuition out of other funds in the future. For one, you may not live long enough to pay the tuition, and the funds you intend to target for education funding thus become subject to tax in your estate. You may be better off by funding the 529 plan and removing mortality risk as a factor.

Furthermore, you may decide that there is little harm done by funding a 529 account and later deciding to make direct tuition payments from other resources in lieu of distributions from the 529 account. An overfunded 529 account can be redirected to another beneficiary in the family, or simply refunded subject to income tax and the 10 percent penalty.

You may even have a case for arguing that the distribution of funds from a 529 plan to the beneficiary is a qualified distribution, even if tuition is paid directly from non-529 sources. The beneficiary would simply receive the distributed 529 funds without tax or penalty, to be used for any purpose. This argument rests on the fact that Section 529 contains no "tracing" rules. However, the IRS may in the future seek to impose rules restricting the free movement of 529 funds in this manner.

What happens if I am making other direct gifts to the beneficiary?

Before funding a 529 account, be sure to count up your other annual-exclusion gifts to that beneficiary. These gifts reduce the amount of annual exclusion that you can apply to 529 contributions. For example, if you normally make a cash gift of $2,000 each year to your grandchild, you will have only $13,000 left in your 2018 annual exclusion. You should limit your 529 contribution under the five-year election to $75,000 unless you are willing to exceed the exclusion amount and use part of your $11.18 million lifetime exemption.

How do I make the five-year election?

You are required to file Form 709 Gift (and Generation-Skipping Transfer) Tax Return in any year that you wish to make the five-year election for your contributions to 529 plans. Form 709 is due on April 15, just like your federal income tax return, but is filed separate from your Form 1040. Make your election by checking Box B on Schedule A of Form 709. Attach an explanation to the return stating the beneficiary's name, your total 529 contributions on behalf of the beneficiary, and the amount for which the election is made.

You need only file Form 709 in the year of election. You will not have to file it for each subsequent year of the election period as long as you have no taxable gifts or generation-skipping transfers to report in those years.

If you and your spouse agree to split your gifts, one-half of your 529 plan contributions will be considered made by each of you. The five-year election, if desired by both spouses, must be made on separate gift-tax returns. Gift splitting can help keep your 529 contributions under the $15,000 annual exclusion amount (or the $75,000 five-year averaging maximum) when you and your spouse do not make equal contributions for a particular beneficiary. See the Form 709 instructions for information on the gift-splitting election.

If my child's grandparent makes contributions to a 529 account on which I am account owner, who has made the gift to my child, the grandparent or me?

Although the IRS has not yet ruled on this particular question, the gift appears to be from the contributor—the grandparent in this case—to the designated beneficiary, even if the contributor is not the account owner. Because the contributor will not retain the rights of ownership in this situation, he or she should consider establishing his or her own account instead. Some grandparents do not desire ownership and prefer to leave responsibility for the 529 account to the beneficiary's parents. In fact, it may help prevent any future problems if the grandparent ends up requiring long-term care and applying for Medicaid benefits.

What happens if the designated beneficiary dies?

Most 529 plans provide that upon the beneficiary's death, the account owner can either direct a distribution to the beneficiary's estate or substitute a new qualifying family member for the deceased beneficiary and continue the account. If nonqualified distributions are made to the beneficiary's estate, or to a substitute beneficiary, the earnings are taxable to that recipient but the 10 percent penalty tax is waived.

The IRS' 1998 proposed regulations suggest the value of the account is included in the deceased beneficiary's gross estate, despite the fact that he or she never had any control or ownership of that asset. Some tax attorneys argue that a beneficiary's gross estate should include the 529 account only where the beneficiary has rights of ownership, e.g. where the beneficiary is also the account owner.

Any future regulations are expected to contain different rules, according to the Advance Notice of Proposed Rulemaking issued by the IRS in January 2008:

♦ The distribution of the entire account to the estate of the beneficiary within six months of death will result in the inclusion of the account in the deceased beneficiary's gross estate.

♦ A change in designated beneficiary to a new beneficiary who is a member of the family of the deceased beneficiary and in the same or higher generation will result in the account not being included in the deceased beneficiary's gross estate.

♦ The distribution of all or part of the account to the account owner, or the failure of the account owner to name a new beneficiary by the due date for filing the deceased beneficiary's estate tax return, will result in the account not being included in the deceased beneficiary's gross estate. The account owner will be liable for income tax on the earnings distributed or deemed distributed.

Most beneficiaries of 529 accounts are young family members with few assets, so the inclusion of the asset value in the estate will usually not create a tax problem.

Other issues to be resolved

There remain a number of other questions regarding the Section 529 gift and estate tax rules that were not adequately addressed by the IRS' 1998 proposed regulations. These include the following:

♦ What are the gift-tax consequences when the account owner, rather than the beneficiary, receives a distribution out of a 529 account? Nothing in the proposed regulations suggests that the beneficiary reports a gift back to the account owner; nor does it appears that the initial gift, recorded at the time of contribution, is canceled or reversed. If the account owner takes the refund proceeds and re-invests in another 529 account for the same beneficiary, assuming it is not a rollover, he or she has apparently made a second gift with essentially the same dollars.

♦ Is there a gift-tax consequence to a transfer of account ownership? A literal reading of Code Section 529 indicates there is not. However, an estate reduction strategy involving the transfer of 529 account ownership, followed by a distribution to the new account owner, will be deemed abusive. See chapter 12 for more discussion.

♦ Assume a contributor dies after making the five-year averaging election, and is required to include a portion of the contributions in his or her gross estate. Can the marital deduction be applied to reduce the taxable estate if account ownership is left to the contributor's spouse? You'll have to rely on an attorney's advice.

NINE

529 Plans vs. Coverdell ESAs

The Coverdell education savings account, known until mid–2001 as the Education IRA, is a direct competitor to the 529 plan, each providing families of the college-bound the opportunity for tax-free earnings. Major improvements were made to the ESA beginning with the 2002 tax year, including an increased annual contribution limit as well as the removal of a provision that prevented families from claiming the tax benefits of ESA distributions and Hope or Lifetime Learning credits in the same year. Further, the list of qualifying expense was expanded beyond college to include primary and secondary school ("K–12") expenses, a change championed by the late Senator Paul Coverdell.

Whereas the "old" Education IRA was not easy to recommend, the new Coverdell ESA is attractive to many parents, especially those intending to send their children to private schools for grades K–12. Although many of its improvements were scheduled to expire at the end of 2012, the American Taxpayer Relief Act of 2012 made them permanent. However, in 2017, the Tax Cuts and Jobs Act expanded the qualified expenses for 529 plans to include up to $10,000 annually in private K-12 tuition, reducing one of the key advantages of the Coverdell ESA.

What is a Coverdell education savings account?

A Coverdell ESA is a trust or custodial account created exclusively to pay the qualified education expenses of a named beneficiary. Banks, savings and loan associations, brokerage firms and mutual fund companies offer Coverdell ESAs in addition to traditional IRAs and Roth IRAs. However, a Coverdell ESA does not require that the contributor have earned income, and does not impact your ability to contribute to a traditional or Roth IRA. Annual contributions to Coverdell ESAs may not exceed $2,000 per child and, unless the child has "special needs," may not be made after the child reaches age 18. The $2,000 contribution limit is applied on a calendar-year basis across all Coverdell ESAs for the same child. You have until April 15 to make contributions counted towards the previous year's $2,000 limit. A special provision enacted in 2008 for families of soldiers killed in action permits the rollover of a Military Death Gratuity to a Coverdell ESA without regard for the $2,000 annual contribution limit.

Any individual, including your child, can contribute to a Coverdell ESA as long as the contributor's modified adjusted gross income (MAGI) is less than $110,000 ($220,000 if filing a joint return).[1] An individual's ability to contribute up to $2,000 for any child is reduced on a ratable basis as modified AGI rises above $95,000, and is phased out completely at $110,000. For joint filers the phase-out range is $190,000 to $220,000. If you are above the income limits, there is nothing to prevent you from making a gift to someone else—probably the child—who is within the limits, followed by a contribution of your gifted funds into the Coverdell ESA. A corporation that makes contributions to a Coverdell ESA is not subject to the income limits.

What is the federal income tax treatment of a Coverdell ESA?

Although your contributions to a Coverdell ESA are not tax-deductible, any withdrawals from the account are exempt from federal tax to the extent the

---

1. MAGI means the adjusted gross income increased by certain exclusions relating to income earned abroad or received from certain American territories or possessions.

beneficiary incurs qualified education expenses during the year. Qualified education expenses include qualified higher education expenses (QHEE) and qualified elementary and secondary education expenses (QESEE). See chapter 3 for the definition of QHEE. QHEE must be reduced by any other tax-free educational benefits, including scholarship and fellowship grants and employer-provided educational assistance.

The following three categories of elementary and secondary school expenses are included in QESEE:

1) tuition, fees, academic tutoring, special needs services in the case of a special needs beneficiary, books, supplies, and other equipment which are incurred in connection with the enrollment or attendance of the designated beneficiary;

2) room and board, uniforms, transportation, and supplementary items and services (including extended day programs) which are required or provided by the school in connection with such enrollment or atten- dance; and

3) any computer technology or equipment or Internet access and related services, if such technology, equipment, or services are to be used by the beneficiary and the beneficiary's family during any of the years the beneficiary is in school.

If withdrawals from a Coverdell ESA exceed the qualified education expenses incurred by the beneficiary during the year, the earnings portion of the excess withdrawal is includable in the beneficiary's gross income, and an additional 10 percent penalty tax is imposed on the earnings. The earnings portion is computed by the beneficiary in the same manner that a 529 plan administrator computes the earnings portion of a 529 account distribution (see chapter 3). IRS Publication 970 (available at www.irs. gov) contains complete instructions for computing the earnings portion of withdrawals and maintaining a record of the tax basis of the account. In 2003, the IRS changed the form used for reporting Coverdell ESA withdrawals to the same form (Form 1099-Q) used for reporting 529 dis- tributions, and proposed that the Coverdell ESA provider, rather than the individual taxpayer, keep track of tax basis. However, in Notice 2003–53, the IRS gave Coverdell administrators a reprieve by permitting Forms 1099-Q to be filed showing only gross distributions and the value of the account, and not requiring a breakdown between earnings and basis. At the time this book went to press, the reprieve was still in place.

The 10 percent penalty tax is computed on Form 5329 and paid with the beneficiary's federal income tax return. Exceptions to the penalty exist for withdrawals made on account of the beneficiary's death, disability, or receipt of a tax-free scholarship (to the extent of the scholarship value).

A state is not required to follow the federal rules described above for purposes of the state income tax, although it appears that every state except Pennsylvania currently conforms to federal treatment of the Coverdell ESA.

What is the federal gift and estate tax treatment of a Coverdell ESA?

Just like contributions to a 529 account, your contributions to a Coverdell ESA are considered completed gifts from you to the beneficiary and are eligible for the gift tax annual exclusion. Because the annual Coverdell ESA contribution limit is below the gift tax annual exclusion amount, the special five-year election (see chapter 8) normally does not come into play. However, in the rare instance where the beneficiary of the Coverdell ESA is changed to a lower-generation family member, the deemed gift rule described for 529 plans applies, and the five-year election is available if the balance at the time of the change exceeds the gift tax annual exclusion amount.

What happens if the account is not spent by the time the beneficiary graduates from college?

Any balance left in a Coverdell ESA when the beneficiary turns age 30 must be distributed within 30 days. The earnings portion is subject to income tax and the 10 percent penalty tax. The age limit does not apply to "special needs beneficiaries." Subject to the policies of the financial institution serving as trustee or custodian of the Coverdell ESA, a change in designated beneficiary may be made before age 30 without incurring tax or penalty, as long as the new beneficiary is a member of the family and under the age of 30. The definition of "member of the family" follows the definition contained in Section 529 (see chapter 3). A rollover of a withdrawal from a Coverdell ESA within 60 days into another Coverdell ESA for the beneficiary or member of the beneficiary's family under the age of 30 is permitted, but only once in a 12-month period.

A balance in a Coverdell ESA may also be withdrawn tax-free and penalty-free in a year when equal or greater contributions are made to a 529 plan for the same beneficiary. This option provides you with significant flexibility if you start out investing with a Coverdell ESA and later decide that you are better off in a 529 plan. It can also extend the deferral of earnings beyond age 30.

Who makes the decisions about investments, withdrawals, and beneficiary changes in a Coverdell ESA?

These aspects are governed by the adoption agreement used by the Coverdell ESA trustee or custodian. The IRS has made available two "model" agreements for use by financial institutions, Form 5305-EA for custodial accounts and Form 5305-E for trust accounts. Since the Coverdell ESA is established for a minor, a "responsible individual" must be named to the account. Forms 5305-EA and 5305-E generally require that the responsible individual be the beneficiary's parent or legal guardian (presumably to guard against multiple account contributions that exceed the $2,000 annual limit). However, the custodian or trustee may establish policies that permit someone besides a parent or guardian to be the responsible individual.

The contributor who opens the account makes the initial investment selection and names the responsible individual. He or she also indicates whether the responsible individual is permitted to change the designated beneficiary to another qualifying family member, and whether control of the account passes to the beneficiary when he or she reaches the legal age of majority. After the account is established, the responsible individual makes decisions as to investments, withdrawals, and beneficiary changes.

Which is better—the 529 plan or the Coverdell ESA?

Ignoring other investment alternatives, any family saving for a child's college education must decide whether their first $2,000 of savings goes into a 529 plan or into a Coverdell ESA. (Beyond $2,000 in annual contributions, the Coverdell ESA is generally not an option.) Factors to consider include the following:

- ♦ **K–12 expenses.** Both a 529 plan and a Coverdell ESA can be withdrawn tax-free for qualifying elementary and secondary school expenses. Coverdell ESAs, however, have a wider definition of qualified elementary and secondary school expenses: a tax-free distribution from 529 plan may only be used for up to $10,000 in tuition costs, and not any other expenses. A family planning to send a child to a private school may find this feature of the Coverdell ESA very attractive. Even for children who will be attending public grade schools, the ability to use the Coverdell ESA for home computer purchases and certain other expenses may be seen as a significant advantage. Anyone home schooling his or her children must be careful; some states do not recognize this type of education as a "school."
- ♦ **Investment options and flexibility.** The financial institution that serves as custodian or trustee of a Coverdell ESA can offer the same types of investments found in individual retirement accounts (IRA), including self-directed investment accounts. Contributions may not be invested in life insurance. You may roll assets from one Coverdell ESA to another Coverdell ESA only once in a 12-month period, but the law does not restrict the number or frequency of investment changes within your current Coverdell ESA. The menu of investment options available in a 529 plan is more limited and you are permitted

only two investment changes or reallocations within a 529 account in any calendar year.

♦ **Fees and expenses.** Because Coverdell ESAs generally require less effort to administer, expenses are often lower than with an equivalent amount invested in a 529 plan. Fees can vary significantly from one ESA sponsor to another, however.

♦ **Account ownership.** In nearly all 529 plans, you remain the owner of the account and can revoke it at any time. That is not the case with Coverdell ESAs. Distributions from a Coverdell ESA are paid directly to the beneficiary or to a guardian on behalf of the beneficiary, and should not revert to the contributor or responsible individual. If the beneficiary of a Coverdell ESA dies, the account is paid out to the beneficiary's estate unless another qualifying family member is substituted as beneficiary.

♦ **Financial aid.** Coverdell ESAs and 529s are treated alike in the federal financial aid formula (see chapter 4). Beginning with the 2009–10 award year, if owned by a dependent student, the account value is reportable on that student's FAFSA as a parent asset, representing a significant advantage over bank accounts and other types of student-owned investments. If owned by an independent student, the Coverdell ESA or 529 account is reportable on the FAFSA as the student's asset.[2]

♦ **State tax benefits.** Your state may offer you a state income tax deduction for some or even all of your contributions to a 529 plan. Currently, there are no states permitting a deduction for Coverdell ESA contributions.

♦ **Excise tax.** If contributions to all Coverdell ESAs for a child exceed $2,000 in a year—or are made after the child reaches age 18 or by a taxpayer who is not eligible based on modified adjusted gross income— the excess contributions are subject to a 6 percent excise tax for each year until corrected. The excise tax is computed on Form 5329 and is filed alone or, if the child is required to file an income tax return, with

---

2. Who "owns" a Coverdell ESA? Unlike a 529 account, which clearly has an owner separate and distinct from the beneficiary, a Coverdell ESA is maintained by an institutional custodian or trustee on behalf of the beneficiary, similar to an UGMA or UTMA account, suggesting that the student is the owner of the ESA in every case. The person named as "responsible individual" has no rights to the Coverdell ESA other than the right to direct investments and, in some accounts, to change beneficiaries.

the child's Form 1040. An excess contribution can be corrected for the year in which it arises by removing the contribution, along with all earnings attributable to the contribution, by May 31 of the year following the year of contribution. The earnings portion of a corrective withdrawal is subject to tax on the child's tax return for the taxable year for which the contribution was made, but the 10 percent penalty is not imposed. An uncorrected excess contribution will be treated as a new contribution in the following year. With a 529 plan, the investor need not worry about federal penalties on excess contributions. Rather, the programs themselves will establish and monitor contribution limits. Any contributions beyond those limits will not be accepted by the 529 plan, or will be returned when discovered, but in any event will not subject the plan participant to a penalty.

- **Tax reporting**. With both the Coverdell ESA and 529 plans, the taxpayer determines the tax treatment of distributions and maintains records of qualifying expenses in the event of an IRS audit. The 529 plan administrator will keep track of your basis and compute the earnings portion of distributions when it reports them on Form 1099-Q. But with a Coverdell ESA, you may need to keep track of basis yourself. The IRS has proposed a change that would require Coverdell ESA administrators to keep track of basis, but has postponed the implementation of that change.

- **Asset protection.** The Bankruptcy Abuse Prevention and Consumer Protection Act of 2005 extended special protections to Coverdell ESAs and to 529 plans. The entire account[3] is exempt from the bankruptcy estate for assets contributed at least two years prior to the bankruptcy filing, while a maximum $5,000 is exempt for assets contributed between one and two years prior to filing. The account beneficiary must be a child, stepchild, grandchild, or step-grandchild of the debtor. In non-bankruptcy actions, assets in Coverdell ESAs may be better protected from creditors than assets in 529 accounts. Speak to your attorney about the laws in your state, and if you invest in an out-of-state 529 plan, how any special protections in that state might apply to you.

---

3. The bankruptcy exclusion cannot exceed the amount needed to provide for the beneficiary's qualified higher education expenses, subject to a cost-of-living adjustment.

✦ **Transfer of assets.** An advantage of the Coverdell ESA is that you can transfer Coverdell ESA assets to a 529 account without federal tax. You cannot transfer tax-free from a 529 plan to a Coverdell ESA. You may even plan for future ESA-to-529 transfers at the time you fund a Coverdell ESA. For example, in order to maximize state tax benefits in a state that caps its annual deduction for contributions to its 529 plan, you may decide to "park" your savings beyond the deduction amount in a Coverdell ESA until a later year when the transfer of those savings into the 529 plan will yield a state tax deduction. The untaxed earnings portion of the Coverdell ESA withdrawal will be recorded as earnings in your 529 account and reported as such when future distributions are made from the 529 plan. To take advantage of the ability to transfer Coverdell ESA assets, you are required to provide the 529 plan administrator with documentation that shows the earnings portion of the Coverdell ESA withdrawal.

Can I regain direct ownership of the assets in my child's Coverdell ESA by transferring these assets to my 529 account, as long as I name my child the beneficiary of the 529 account?

Although you satisfy the literal requirements for a tax-free and penalty-free transfer, you may be violating state laws designed to protect the ownership rights of your child in the Coverdell ESA. This situation is similar to assets that are owned by a minor through a custodial arrangement (UTMA or UGMA). Seek the advice of your attorney in this situation as you may be required by law to establish the 529 account in such a way as to protect the minor's ownership rights.

TEN

529 Plans vs. U.S. Savings Bonds

Under certain conditions, an owner of U.S. savings bonds may redeem those bonds and exclude the interest from income if the proceeds are used for qualified higher education expenses. These rules are contained in Section 135 of the Internal Revenue Code. Eligible bonds include Series EE bonds issued after 1989 and all Series I bonds, but only when purchased by an individual who was at least 24 years old on the first day of the month in which the bond was purchased. These eligible bonds are sometimes referred to as education savings bonds.

Savings bonds are attractive to many savers because they are backed by the full faith and credit of the U.S. government, their interest is exempt from state and local income taxes, and they are easy to purchase. Electronic bonds can be purchased directly over the Internet (www.savingsbonds. gov). They are issued in face values as low as $25. In the past, paper EE bonds were sold by financial institutions at one-half their face value, but as of January 1, 2012 paper EE bonds are no longer available.

There are limits on how much you may invest in savings bonds in any particular year. The maximum annual investment is $10,000 for electronic

Series I bonds, and $10,000 for electronic Series EE bonds. Paper I bonds may be purchased using your IRS tax refund, but are issued with a $50 minimum denomination and are subject to a $5,000 annual maximum purchase.

A Series EE bond purchased today will earn interest at a fixed rate, with rates for new issues adjusted each May 1 and November 1. Accrued interest is added to the value of the bond. EE bonds issued before May 1, 2005 are subject to different terms.

Series I bonds (known simply as I Bonds) were first issued in September 1998 and are also sold at face value. Interest is composed of a fixed rate of return plus a variable semiannual inflation rate based on the Consumer Price Index. The 30-year fixed rate on I Bonds issued between May 1, 2018 and October 1, 2018 is 0.30%. These particular bonds have an initial composite annual earnings rate of 2.52%, but adjust on each 6-month and 12-month anniversary of the issue date for a new inflation figure. The issue date is the first day of the month in which the bond was purchased.

Series EE and I bonds earn interest for up to 30 years and are redeemable after twelve months, although you forfeit three months of interest if you redeem a bond within five years of its issuance.

In order to exclude any bond interest under the Section 135 education exclusion, your income must be below a certain level in the year of redemption. In 2015, the exclusion is phased out for joint filers and surviving spouses with modified adjusted gross income between $117,250 and $147,250. The phase-out range for single taxpayers is $78,150 to $93,150. These limitations are adjusted each year for inflation. Note that your income, for purposes of the limitation, includes the entire amount of interest on redeemed savings bonds without regard to the potential exclusion. Married taxpayers filing separately do not qualify for the education exclusion.

For many taxpayers, it will be difficult to predict future income levels at the time of a bond purchase, so the bond owner may end up not being able to take the tax break anticipated at purchase. The rule requiring that you be at least 24 years old is designed to prevent you from avoiding the income limitation through issuance of bonds directly in your child's name.

The entire amount of bond redemption proceeds is compared to qualified higher education expenses in determining the amount of interest excluded from your gross income. If the redemption proceeds exceed qualifying expenses, the amount of excludable interest is reduced pro rata. The exclusion is figured on Form 8815, to be filed with your Form 1040 for the year you redeem the bonds.

"Qualified higher educational expenses" are defined differently for the bond income exclusion than for 529 plans and Coverdell education savings accounts. For the bond income exclusion, qualified higher education expenses include only tuition and fees for the bond owner or the bond owner's spouse or dependent. (A grandparent will not be able to take advantage of the exclusion except in the unusual situation where the child is the grandparent's dependent.) Also treated as qualified expenses are contributions made to a 529 plan or Coverdell ESA that names you, your spouse or your dependent as beneficiary. Qualified expenses exclude any costs for sports, games, or hobbies, unless they are incurred as part of a degree program. Total qualified expenses must be reduced by the tuition used in determining the American Opportunity credit or Lifetime Learning credit, by tax-exempt scholarships, and by qualified distributions from a 529 plan or Coverdell ESA.

For the college saver who appreciates the investment characteristics of savings bonds, this set of rules makes planning interesting, to say the least. And to use the bonds in conjunction with a 529 plan or Coverdell ESA is particularly challenging. After reducing your child's total tuition and related expenses by your 529 plan and Coverdell ESA distributions, there will likely be little, if any, qualified expenses to use against bond redemption proceeds. It appears the tax coordination rules will not permit you to attach your 529/ESA distributions first to non-tuition, qualified higher education expenses, such as room and board, leaving the tuition and fees for use against bond redemption proceeds.

Which is better for college savings—savings bonds or a 529 plan?

If you have to choose, the 529 plan will be the preferred vehicle for many, although a number of variables should be considered. Certainly, your anticipated future income level is an important factor because the tax break on savings bond redemptions is lost for higher-income taxpayers. If you own savings bonds but never find a way to fit within the education exclusion, the interest will be subject to federal income tax (but not state income tax) when you redeem the bonds. Your income level will not prevent you from taking advantage of the tax exclusion on 529 plan distributions.

Another obvious consideration is the gross investment return available from a U.S. savings bond versus a 529 plan. Over a long investment horizon, a 529 savings account invested in a portfolio of equity and debt securities is likely to outperform a savings bond. But the level of market risk is higher, too. A conservative investor may be more attracted to savings bonds no matter how long the targeted investment horizon happens to be, but that investor could also choose a 529 savings plan with an option that guarantees principal and interest.

A 529 prepaid program will outperform a savings bond if the value of benefits under the contract, based on future tuition increases, exceeds the interest earnings on the bond. Recent history has shown tuition inflation on average to be significantly higher than increases in the Consumer Price Index. Whether the interest premium on savings bonds, if any (the fixed rate on I Bonds purchased from November 2014 through April 2015 is zero), can close the tuition inflation gap is a question that has no certain answer.

Yet another variable is the amount of money you have available for investment. A 529 savings program can be used for certain educational expenses, such as room and board, that savings bonds cannot cover under the education exclusion.

I already have a significant investment in eligible U.S. savings bonds, but I am interested in 529 plans too. What are my options?

Since it is difficult to effectively combine the tax exclusion for savings bonds with other education tax incentives, you need to decide whether the bond education exclusion is your best bet. Fortunately, you may not need to make this decision now. The tax law permits you to claim the education exclusion on your redemption of qualifying savings bonds to the extent contributions are made to a 529 plan or Coverdell ESA that names you, your spouse, or your dependent as beneficiary. In essence, the contribution to a 529 plan or Coverdell ESA constitutes a qualified higher education expense for purposes of the education savings bond exclusion. It is important to remember, however, that you must satisfy the income requirements in the year of redemption in order to take advantage of the opportunity.

The ability to make this transfer out of savings bonds without triggering tax provides a significant degree of flexibility. In fact, you may decide to purchase qualifying savings bonds with the intent of making the transfer to a 529 plan or ESA in a future year.

Here are some situations in which the transfer should be considered:

- You currently own qualifying U.S. savings bonds and your income is within the limits this year, but the bonds are targeted for college expenses in a future year, and you expect your income to be too high in that year. By redeeming the bonds now and transferring the proceeds into a 529 plan or Coverdell ESA, you succeed in "locking in" the tax exclusion on bond interest no matter what your income level is in the future. However, the strategy will backfire if you end up taking nonqualified distributions from your 529 account after transferring the bond proceeds into the account. Not only will the deferred bond interest become subject to tax, but it will incur the 10 percent penalty tax as well.

- Similarly, you may be unsure of your ability to claim the future college student as your dependent under the various dependency tests. You may decide to make the tax-free transfer from savings bonds to a 529 plan this year while your child still qualifies as a dependent. With a 529 plan, the dependency status of your child should no longer matter.

- You intend to use your qualifying savings bonds to pay college expenses for a currently enrolled child. Even though your income is within the bond exclusion limits, you discover that you will not be able to take full advantage of the exclusion because you lack sufficient qualified expenses. This can easily occur, for instance, when the tuition is absorbed by the American Opportunity or Lifetime Learning credit, or when it is reduced by qualified distributions from a 529 plan or Coverdell ESA. You will save taxes by first directing the bond redemption proceeds to a 529 plan or Coverdell ESA and then taking distributions for college expenses. Section 529 plan and Coverdell ESA withdrawals can be used to pay for certain expenses (i.e. room and board, books, supplies, and equipment) that are not considered qualified expenses under the education bond exclusion.

♦ Because Coverdell ESAs can be used for certain elementary and secondary school expenses that are not counted for the education bond exclusion, the transfer of bond redemption proceeds into a Coverdell ESA for this purpose may offer an added benefit.

I am a grandparent who owns post–1989 savings bonds and I would like to use these bonds to pay for my grandchild's college costs. Can I take advantage of the education bond exclusion?

Unfortunately, unless your grandchild is also your dependent, you do not qualify for the education bond exclusion. You will have to report the interest income on your tax return in the year you redeem the bonds even if you use the proceeds to fund a 529 plan or Coverdell ESA for the grandchild. However, there appears to be a loophole if you establish a 529 account, naming yourself as beneficiary, and redeeming eligible bonds to fund that account. You meet the literal requirements for the education bond exclusions by naming yourself beneficiary of the 529 account. Sometime later, you change the beneficiary of the 529 account to your grandchild. Be sure to discuss this strategy with your own tax professional before attempting it.

Why should I worry about qualifying for the education bond exclusion when I can avoid tax by purchasing the bonds in my child's name and reporting the accrued interest on her tax return each year?

This alternative strategy no longer works as well as it used to. Although by adopting this method of reporting your child can effectively shelter the annual bond interest accrual with her standard deduction (the greater of $1,050 or the sum of $350 and the individual's earned income in 2018), if she is subject to the kiddie tax any unearned income in excess of twice her standard deduction will be taxed at your marginal tax rate. The kiddie tax now affects children as old as 23 (see chapter 11). Your decision to report your child's accruing bond interest each year on her tax return applies to all future years unless you receive permission from the IRS to begin deferring the interest.

Also be sure to consider other aspects of placing investments in the name of your child, such as gift-tax consequences and student financial-aid impact.

Some parents who otherwise qualify for the education bond exclusion discover too late that the savings bonds were originally issued in the child's name, violating the requirement that the bonds be issued to an individual at least 24 years old. If they do not elect annual reporting of interest, the entire amount of accrued interest is taxable to the child upon redemption. It may be possible, however, to re-register the bonds in the name of the parent. Go to www.savingsbonds.gov for more information about correcting mistakes in the registration of your bonds. Also see IRS Publication 550, available online at www.irs.gov.

ELEVEN

529 Plans vs. Other Investment Alternatives

Besides 529 plans, Coverdell education savings accounts, and U.S. savings bonds, a number of other tax strategies and financial products have been popular over the years among families seeking to save for future college costs. While these alternatives may not be directly or exclusively geared to college savings, they are easily adapted for this purpose. This chapter will discuss several of these options in comparison to the 529 plan.

IRA Withdrawals Used for Higher Education Expenses

Before the Taxpayer Relief Act of 1997, an IRA withdrawal taken before the owner turned 59½ years of age and used to pay for education expenses would incur a 10 percent penalty on premature distributions. The changes made in 1997 now allow a premature IRA distribution to be taken without penalty if used to pay for the qualified higher education expenses of the taxpayer or the taxpayer's spouse, child, or grandchild. Qualified higher education expenses include the same categories of expense applicable to 529 distributions, but are reduced by the proceeds from the tax-free redemption of qualified U.S. savings bonds.

Many individuals have assets in individual retirement accounts and it is nice to know that those assets are accessible not only for retirement, but also in the event they are needed for college expenses. Note, however, that any *earnings* in an IRA will still be taxable when withdrawn for college. The *principal* portion of a distribution from a traditional IRA will also be taxable to the extent you claimed deductions for your contributions to the IRA.

A Roth IRA can be more effective than a traditional IRA when tapped for college expenses. Because contributions to a Roth IRA are not deductible, the principal will always come out tax-free. Best of all, Roth IRA distributions are first considered a nontaxable return of principal; earnings come out only after the principal is exhausted. A viable strategy is to withdraw principal for college expenses and leave the earnings to grow in the Roth IRA. Once you turn 59½ and have held the Roth IRA for at least five years, all distributions, including earnings, are tax-free.

Which investment vehicle should I use—an IRA or a 529 plan?

For many people, the answer would be the IRA, and more specifically, the Roth IRA. The Roth IRA offers federal income tax benefits equivalent to the 529 plan—even better, if you qualify for the Saver's Credit.[1] In addition, the Roth IRA withdrawn in retirement can be used for any purpose without negative consequences, whereas the 529 plan is tax-free only if used to pay qualified higher education expenses. Consider also that for many people the objective of funding retirement is a higher priority than

---

1. The federal Saver's Credit is targeted to low and moderate income taxpayers making contributions to a qualified retirement plan (e.g. 401k) or IRA. The credit is worth 50%, 20%, or 10%—depending on income level—of the taxpayer's contributions in any year, with a maximum annual credit of $2,000 ($4,000 for joint filers). In order to claim the credit, the taxpayer must be at least 18 years old but cannot be a full-time student or the tax dependent of another taxpayer. A single taxpayer must have income below $31,500 to claim the credit in 2018, and a married couple filing jointly must have income below $63,000.

funding college. Borrowing is almost always an option for college expenses but not for retirees with inadequate financial resources.

So why not forget about the 529 plan and just concentrate on using the Roth IRA? If you are not already contributing the maximum amount to a Roth IRA, perhaps you should. But the Roth IRA is subject to income limitations, just like the Coverdell ESA. Furthermore, the annual contribution limit in 2018 is only $5,500 ($6,500 under a catch-up provision for anyone age 50 and above). It also requires that you have earned income at least equal to the amount of the contribution.

For federal financial-aid purposes, an IRA or Roth IRA is a mixed blessing. The IRA balance will not be counted as part of the expected family contribution. But if IRA withdrawals were taken during the previous year, the financial aid application requires that any untaxed principal, in addition to taxable earnings that show up on the Form 1040, be added to the student's or parents' income in the formula.

You will probably find that the IRA is not the total solution to saving for your child's college expenses. Even if it were large enough to cover the cost, tapping it for college means it will not be there for your retirement. A 529 plan will probably still provide the best means to save for the largest portion of future college expenses.

Should I be funding a 529 account instead of making contributions to my employer's 401(k) plan?

Unlike an IRA, a 401(k) cannot be tapped directly for college expenses before you retire. If the plan permits you to take a loan, you could use the loan proceeds to pay college expenses, but the loan must be repaid.

Choosing between a 529 plan and your employer's 401(k) plan will depend on your own particular circumstances. As discussed above, the importance of saving for retirement may turn out to be your overriding concern and you will want to maximize any opportunity you have to contribute to qualified retirement plans. An analysis of your current and projected future tax situation can also help in your decision. With a 401(k) you are making "pre-tax" contributions—i.e. you receive an upfront tax break on your contributions—but you pay income tax down the road on the full amount of each distribution. Similar to a Roth IRA, contributions to a 529 plan are made with after-tax dollars, and qualified distributions are tax-free.

If your state offers a tax deduction for contributions into its 529 plan, you may decide that is reason enough to direct some dollars into that program. However, in most cases it will be unwise to do so if it means you will be giving up an employer match of your 401(k) contributions.

Investments in Your Child's Name

Traditional investment planning for college-bound families often includes the transfer of income-producing assets from parent to child in order to take advantage of the child's low tax bracket. When the child is under 24 years old, this planning must consider the impact of the so-called "kiddie tax." If the child is subject to the kiddie tax, investment income above $2,100 (in 2018) is taxed at the rates that apply to estates and trusts:

Up to $2,500	10%
$2,500 to $9,150	24%
$9,150 to $12,500	35%
Over $12,500	37%

The first $1,050 of the child's investment income is fully sheltered by the standard deduction and the next $1,050 is taxed at the lowest 10 percent income tax bracket. IRS Form 8615 is used to compute the kiddie tax.

Before 2008, the kiddie tax was no longer imposed once the child reached age 18. But now it can affect individuals as old as 23 (see box on page 147). If your child has taxable investments, liquidating those investments for college and triggering capital gains may result in a tax liability based on your capital gains rate (probably 20%) rather than your child's capital gains rate (possibly 0%). Thus the decades-old strategy of gifting large amounts of money or investment securities to your child as a way to save taxes is no longer very effective.

Gifting assets to your child can also hurt his or her financial aid eligibility. As discussed in chapter 4, a student's investment assets—other than a 529 plan, Coverdell ESA, or IRA—are counted heavily in the calculation of the student's expected family contribution, or EFC. Furthermore, when investment assets are sold to pay for college the gain reported on the child's federal income tax return can reduce financial aid eligibility for the following year by as much as 50 percent of the gain.

Kiddie Tax Rules

Congress in 2008 changed the kiddie tax rules, a consequence of ongoing efforts in Washington to raise tax revenues for other initiatives. Individuals subject to the kiddie tax are required to apply their parents' marginal tax rate to unearned income (e.g. interest, dividends, capital gains, and other non-wage income) that exceeds twice the minimum standard deduction amount. In 2018, the minimum standard deduction amount is the greater of $1,050 or the sum of the individual's earned income, placing the kiddie-tax threshold at $2,100. Earned income is not subject to the kiddie tax, and as much as $12,000 in earned income can be sheltered by the child's standard deduction.

Before 2006, the added tax burden was imposed only on children under the age of 14. In May 2006, Congress delayed the age of kiddie-tax emancipation from 14 to 18, retroactive to the beginning of that year. Beginning with 2008, the kiddie tax was expanded once again, to include individuals falling into any one the following three groups (with an exception for those filing a joint return or not having a living parent on the last day of the tax year):

♦ Children age 19 or under

♦ 19-24 year-olds who are full-time students and do not have earned income exceeding one-half of their total support.

Example: Ellen is 16 years old and does not have a job. Her parents had made gifts to a UTMA account for Ellen in previous years and in 2018 the account generates $1,200 in interest income and $3,500 in long-term capital gains. Ellen's parents are in the 35% tax bracket. Ellen is claimed as a dependent on her parent's tax return.

- Under the kiddie-tax rules, the first $1,050 of Ellen's interest income is free from tax, shielded by the standard deduction for a dependent.

- The next $1,050 of investment income is taxed in Ellen's own tax bracket. This consists of the remaining $150 in interest income, taxed at the lowest 10% ordinary-income rate, and $900 of capital gains, which is taxed at 0% under the special rate for capital gains applicable to taxpayers in the 10% and 15% ordinary-income brackets. The remaining $2,600 of capital gains is taxed at the rates that apply to trusts and estates, which in this case is 24%

- Ellen's total federal tax is $639.

Life Insurance and Annuities

Families are sometimes advised to invest in annuity contracts or life insurance because these assets are generally not reportable on the financial aid application. Life insurance has attractive tax features, including tax-deferred build-up of value and tax-free death benefits. Universal life insurance policies can work especially well as a college savings vehicle. They are flexible and allow parents to adjust the level of premium payments, borrow against cash value, and make partial withdrawals. A related product, variable universal life, allows the policy owner to select the underlying investments from a menu of mutual funds and provides more upside potential in the cash value build-up. If a cash-value policy is used as a college savings vehicle, it is important to start early in the child's life to allow time for the policy to build in value. A careful review of the prospectus is necessary to understand all costs and restrictions.

Annuities are insurance products sometimes chided for their low investment return as affected by mortality and expense charges, as well as for the penalties charged on withdrawal or surrender in the first five to ten years. There is an additional problem for most college parents in that annuity payments received prior to the age of 59½ are subject to a 10 percent federal tax on top of the income tax. A 529 plan will generally provide a better tax outcome when used for college expenses.

Treasury Inflation-Indexed Securities

The U.S. government promotes its Treasury Inflation-Protected Securities (TIPS) as an appropriate investment for college savings. These bonds are sold in $1,000 denominations and the principal value is adjusted upwards each year for inflation as measured by the CPI. TIPS are sold with terms of 5, 10, or 30 years. The bond's redemption value at the end of its term includes the annual inflation adjustments. The coupon rate paid semi-annually on these bonds is lower than a comparable-term regular Treasury bond, but the rate is applied to the inflation-adjusted value, so the interest paid to the bondholder increases each year. Even if you are satisfied with the yield, the tax treatment of these bonds is a disadvantage. Investors must pay federal tax each year not only on the interest payments, but also on the value increase from the inflation adjustment.

The inflation protection offered by TIPS and the tax advantages of a 529 plan might seem like an attractive combination for the safety-conscious investor interested in hedging tuition inflation. In fact, 529 savings programs in several states now offer investment options featuring TIPS, allowing you to take advantage of the benefits while avoiding the tax problems.

Zero Coupon and College Savings Bonds

Zero coupon bonds are bonds that do not pay interest but are issued at a discount to face value. The size of the discount determines the effective interest rate on the bond if held to maturity. Zero coupon bonds can be useful for college saving because maturities can be matched to the college years, and holders do not have to deal with the reinvestment of interest (unlike interest-paying bonds). The price of a zero coupon bond sold prior to maturity is affected not only by the amount of unearned interest, but also by market conditions at the time of sale. In a period of rising interest rates, the relative value of the bond will decrease.

There are several types of zero coupon bonds, each with unique tax and investment characteristics. Zero Coupon Treasury bonds are U.S. Treasury bonds or notes that have been stripped of their coupons and sold at a discount to face value. Corporations issue zero coupon bonds that provide a higher return on investment because they are subject to the risk of default (principal and earned discount could be lost). Banks may issue zero coupon certificates of deposit that are FDIC-insured up to $250,000.

Most zero coupon alternatives, including those mentioned above, suffer a disadvantage: although you don't receive the interest until redemption, you are required to report each year's earned discount in taxable income. Zero coupon municipal bonds do not present this problem because, except for the individual who has to pay state tax on an out-of-state bond, their interest is tax-exempt for federal and state purposes.

Several states have issued bonds that are specifically targeted to families saving for college. These are essentially zero coupon municipal bonds although they are often given the name of college savings bonds, baccalaureate bonds, or similar. There have been few, if any, recent issuances of these bonds due to the popularity of 529 plans.

Mutual Funds

Five main advantages are commonly cited for the use of taxable mutual funds, as opposed to 529 plans, for college savings. They are (1) potential for superior investment performance, (2) ability to direct the investments, (3) low tax rates on capital gains and dividends, (4) lower fees and expenses, and (5) ability to use the investment for any purpose without penalty. Each of these factors is examined below.

The first supposed advantage, potential for superior investment performance, is valid only when comparing taxable mutual funds to the prepaid variety of 529 plan. The 529 savings programs provide the college saver with returns directly linked to the investments in the 529 portfolios, and these investments are often the same equity mutual funds that would be attractive to the non–529 college saver. In fact, they may be even better. Taxable mutual funds are sometimes deliberately managed to achieve a "tax-efficient" result, creating a risk that investment decisions are based on tax considerations. The manager of a 529 savings program has no reason to be concerned with the tax consequences of investment activity and can focus entirely on making the best investment decisions within its asset guidelines and investment policy.

The second noted advantage of taxable mutual funds, the ability to direct investments among different funds at the discretion of the owner, will never be totally matched by 529 plans absent a change to the law. By definition, a 529 plan cannot allow the account owner to direct the investments. In actuality, the increasing number of 529 savings programs, the ever-expanding menu of investment options available, and the ability to change your investment option twice every year or roll over your account to another state's program once every 12 months,[2] together provide as much flexibility as most investors will ever need.

Perhaps more relevant, however, is the question of whether the ability to direct investments is an advantage or a disadvantage. Most states have hired professional money managers for their 529 plans to determine the mix of investments that should produce the best balance of risk and return for any particular beneficiary's college savings. The "age-based" options available in most 529 savings program continue to be the most popular options, offering a mechanism that automatically shifts the account to lower-risk investments as the beneficiary approaches college age, and preventing the novice investor from doing damage to his or her own savings.

---

2. See chapter 3 for a discussion of the additional investment flexibility now permitted

Of course, the age-based approach does not produce an asset allocation and investment approach that takes into account all the other components of your financial situation. A professional investment advisor or financial planner can provide valuable services even if you select the age-based option, and will seek to incorporate the 529 investment into your total financial picture in an effective way.

The third perceived advantage of taxable mutual funds, low tax rates on capital gains and dividends, will generally not stand up to close scrutiny. A 2003 study published by the TIAA-CREF Institute compared after-tax accumulations of an investment in a 529 plan and a portfolio of equivalent investments (stock mutual funds) in a taxable account.[3] Assuming the investor is in the 25% federal tax bracket and a 6% state tax bracket, and that the expenses are the same under both alternatives, the study found that after 18 years the 529 investor winds up with a balance 12% higher than that of the mutual fund investor.

But what about the expenses in a 529 plan (the fourth objection listed above)? Most 529 plans charge management fees and/or account maintenance fees and these charges will reduce your overall investment return. The TIAA-CREF Institute study included a second set of calculations which assumed 529 plan expenses were 0.47% higher than taxable mutual fund expenses. The result: the advantage of the 529 plans over the 18-year investment horizon was reduced from 12% to 8%. But since that study was published, expenses in many 529 plans have dropped to a level well below 0.47%. Also, the study found that the advantage of a state income tax deduction in certain 529 plans can overcome the disadvantage of 529 program expenses.

The fifth objection is the flexibility to use mutual funds for any purpose. An investor withdrawing funds from a 529 plan for a purpose other than college suffers the consequence of reporting the earnings as ordinary income and paying an additional 10 percent penalty tax. In most cases, the investor who ends up using his 529 money for non-educational expenditures would have been better off investing in taxable mutual funds. The risk of winding up in this situation should be assessed prior

---

3. TIAA-CREF Institute, *The 2003 Tax Law's Impact on College Savings Plans, Quarterly (Summer 2003)*

to making the decision to use a 529 plan. If you do use a 529 plan, and ultimately find yourself in the position of withdrawing funds that will not be used for college, you should consider the option of directing the withdrawal to your child, not to yourself, in an effort to lessen the tax cost.

Uniform Gifts or Transfers to Minors Act

The Uniform Gifts to Minors Act (UGMA), adopted in some form in all 50 states, allows assets to be transferred to a custodian for the benefit of a minor child. The child receives direct ownership of the assets upon reaching the age of majority (18 or 21) as determined under state law. The Uniform Transfers to Minors Act (UTMA), a more recent alternative to the UGMA, and available in nearly all states, works in essentially the same manner. The UTMA account is preferable in several respects, because it may stay open for a longer period of time (up to age 25 in some states), and because it can hold certain types of assets, such as real estate interests, that the UGMA account cannot. UGMA/UTMA accounts do not provide the level of control available to the donor in a 529 plan, where assets may be kept out of the hands of the beneficiary indefinitely.

Dividends, interest, or capital gains realized in an UGMA/UTMA account will be taxed to the minor beneficiary and may be subject to the kiddie tax if the child is under age 24. However, the donor, not the child, will recognize the income from an UGMA/UTMA account if it is used to satisfy the donor's legal obligation to support the minor.

You also need to be careful about the estate tax treatment of UGMA/UTMA accounts. While a contribution to a 529 plan is removed from your gross estate, UGMA/UTMA transfers will be included in your gross estate if you die while serving as custodian. To avoid this risk, you would name someone else—perhaps your spouse—as custodian at the time the account is established, thereby relinquishing your control over its management.

Can I transfer my child's existing UGMA/UTMA assets into a 529 plan?

Yes, if you are custodian and decide that a 529 plan is a better way to save, you can liquidate the current investments and reinvest the proceeds in a 529 plan. The sale of investments may generate a tax on capital gains. See checklist item #4 in chapter 6 for a description of the different ways 529 plans accommodate contributions from an existing UGMA/UTMA account. Ultimately, it is your responsibility as custodian to comply with state law in handling UGMA/UTMA funds. Some parents will be disappointed to learn that a transfer of assets to a 529 plan will not result in a transfer of ownership rights from the minor to the parent. The minor will assume direct ownership of the 529 account at the age of majority or other age established under the law. For this reason, consider spending down current UGMA/UTMA assets for the benefit of the minor, and replacing those funds by contributing your own money into a 529 plan. If you do have a 529 account for a minor under the UGMA/UTMA, establish a different account for any of your own funds.

> You can check whether converting your UGMA/UTMA assets to a 529 plan will maximize your savings by visiting Savingforcollege.com/UTMA

Irrevocable Trust

A gift to an irrevocable trust allows you to maintain some level of control over the assets by dictating the terms of the trust agreement. The trust agreement could provide that your beneficiaries will receive trust corpus and income only under certain conditions. However, there are several problems with this approach. Any income retained in the trust is taxed not to you or to the trust beneficiary, but to the trust itself, at tax brackets that escalate very quickly. Also, your transfer to the trust is considered a gift of a "future interest," and does not qualify for the $15,000 gift tax annual exclusion.

You can deal with the gift tax problem by establishing a "Crummey" trust. A Crummey power allows the beneficiary to withdraw the current year's gift within a limited time period, often 30 days following the contribution of funds to the trust. The beneficiary is not expected to exercise this right. When properly drafted and executed, the transfer of property to a Crummey trust qualifies for the $15,000 gift tax annual exclusion as a gift of a present interest. Income generated by the trust may be taxed to the trust, to the beneficiary with Crummey withdrawal rights, or to the distributee of the income, depending on the circumstances.

A 529 plan offers the asset control that individuals establishing Crummey trusts are attempting to achieve, without all the complications. A Crummey trust can invest in life insurance policies, however, which is not possible with 529 plans.

Section 2503(c) Minor's Trust

Another way to qualify the gift-in-trust for the $15,000 gift tax annual exclusion is to establish the trust under Code Section 2503(c). The so-called "minor's trust" provides the trustee total discretion to expend trust corpus and income for the benefit of the minor before he or she turns 21; the beneficiary receives any remaining balance upon reaching age 21. The estate tax and income tax consequences are variable depending on a number of factors. Section 529 plans are better than Section 2503(c) trusts for most college savers.

Section 2503(b) Income Trust

This trust requires all income to be distributed at least annually. The "income interest" will qualify for the $15,000 gift tax annual exclusion as a gift of a present interest, valued under IRS tables, while the "remainder interest" is a gift of a future interest and will not qualify for the annual exclusion. There is no requirement that the trust terminate when the beneficiary turns 21. Again, the 529 plan is superior to the 2503(b) trust in that the entire interest may be retained in the 529 plan until you decide to withdraw it, the earnings are tax-deferred and potentially tax free, and the entire contribution (not just the income interest) qualifies for the gift tax annual exclusion.

Family Partnership

A family partnership or family limited liability company can be formed to hold securities and other investments that may be targeted for college savings or any other purpose. This can be a very useful tool for transferring assets to the next generation and can provide a way to shift income, reduce a large estate, and even provide some level of creditor protection. For gift and estate tax purposes, a valuation discount may be available for the fractional partnership interest gifted to the child. This may of course be challenged by the IRS, which looks for a "business purpose" and has a particular problem with family partnerships consisting only of marketable securities and no other business assets. In addition to all the potential tax advantages of a family partnership, you can also maintain effective control of the portion of the assets that are gifted away by transferring limited partnership interests and retaining the general partnership interest. The general partner has the authority to make decisions for the partnership, including the timing and amount of distributions to the partners.

The disadvantage of family partnerships is that they must be carefully crafted and they require significant effort for annual recordkeeping and tax reporting. In addition, the Internal Revenue Code contains certain income tax provisions targeted directly at family partnerships. A full explanation of the advantages and disadvantages of a family partnership is beyond the scope of this book and anyone interested in this option should consult an attorney. Due to the expense of setting up and maintaining family partnerships, they are usually only recommended when significant assets are at stake. A 529 plan, on the other hand, is a much simpler and much less expensive way to set up a college savings program for your family.

TWELVE

Managing Your 529 Account

A parent—let's call him John—decides to use a 529 plan but wants to keep it as simple as possible. He begins by establishing an investment account, or purchasing a prepaid tuition contract, for each of his children in his state's 529 plan. As the years go by, he pays little attention to the accounts, confident they will be there to help pay for the colleges his children ultimately decide to attend. When the college bills finally roll in, John taps the entire value of each account or prepayment contract for that purpose.

For John, as well as for many others, this uncomplicated approach will produce the desired results, and even the most restrictive 529 plan can be an appropriate choice. Realize, however, that federal tax law offers a significant degree of flexibility to those utilizing 529 plans as a savings vehicle. From a planning perspective, this flexibility can be extremely attractive. It means that you are not locked into the decisions made when the account is first established. As circumstances change, you can make adjustments to ensure that the benefits of your college savings accounts are maximized.

Most 529 plans allow you to change some aspect of your account. Well-timed moves can sometimes save federal and state income taxes, estate taxes, and generation-skipping transfer taxes, and can enhance eligibility for federal financial aid as well. Even if you change nothing substantial, you may still have to make some decisions along the way in order to take full advantage of 529 plans.

The flexibility allowed under federal tax law is not fully incorporated into all 529 plans. As demonstrated in chapter 6, some programs may limit your maneuverability. Understand these limitations before selecting a 529 plan and making contributions.

Basic Account Management

Let's assume that you have decided which 529 plan to use. You used the checklist in chapter 6 or sought the guidance of your financial planner. You've read through the official program materials and understand how the program works. If it is a savings program with different investment options, you have selected the option, or combination of options, that best suits you. What else do you need to think about? There are at least three questions you face between now and the time your child graduates from college.

1) When should you make your contributions?

It may not be wise to throw every available penny into a 529 plan at your first opportunity. You may be able to do better by spreading your contributions over time to obtain the most benefit from your investment and save as much in taxes as possible. Here are some reasons why:

♦ Capital gains tax. If you have to liquidate other investments to fund your 529 account, carefully consider the tax consequences. Properly timing the sale can make a difference in how much income tax you pay. Chapters 7 and 11 cover this topic in more detail.

♦ State tax benefits. If your state offers an income tax deduction for your contributions, or perhaps a matching grant, consider how the timing of your contributions can affect the size of the benefit. For instance, if you live in a state like New York that puts an annual cap on the amount of the deduction you can claim for contributions to its 529 plan, and does not allow you to carry over excess contributions to future years, you may want to spread your contributions over more than one year to capture a greater tax benefit.

♦ Gift tax. If you decide to contribute more than $15,000 to a 529 plan for a particular beneficiary, or if you are making other gifts to that individual, be careful to formulate a gifting strategy. One of your objectives may be to stay within the gift tax annual exclusion. Making the special five-year election may help you do this. For example, if you wish to maximize your contributions while staying within the gift tax annual exclusion amount so as not to use up any of your $11.18 million lifetime exemption, and it is already late in the 2018 year, consider making a $15,000 contribution this year, and waiting until the beginning of next year before contributing another $75,000. By holding off on the five-year election until 2019 you have funded your account with $90,000 in contributions free from the gift tax, rather than $75,000. (However, you will have consumed your annual exclusions going into year six rather than year five.)

♦ Account expenses. Consider how the timing of your contributions might affect your overall program cost. Some of the 529 savings programs charge an annual account maintenance fee, but will waive the fee if you sign up through a payroll deduction plan, agree to automatic monthly or quarterly contributions from your checking or savings account, or maintain a specified minimum account balance. With some prepaid tuition programs, the price of a prepayment contract will vary based on the age of the child, usually with older children being more expensive, but in some programs the opposite being true. Prices of prepayment contracts also usually increase over time, and procrastination can be expensive. However, you could be better off waiting until next year if you determine that the price of a prepayment contract will not increase by very much and you can set the money aside in an interest-earning account in the meantime. In many prepaid programs, you will also need to decide whether to purchase a higher-priced contract under an installment payment plan (total payments will be more than the lump-sum cost of the contract), or a lower-priced contract now with the intent to buy additional semesters or tuition units in future years.

- ♦ Market risk. Investing in a 529 savings program is similar to investing in mutual funds. Although the concepts of modern portfolio theory are beyond the scope of this book, some experts recommend "dollar cost averaging" as a way to manage the risk of a volatile stock market. This involves making contributions at regular intervals. (A number of 529 plans now offer a dollar-cost-averaging mechanism that allows the investor to pre-program the movement of a large initial contribution into equity-based options over time.) Remember also that your college savings accounts are probably just one piece of your total investment "pie" and that you should be balancing your asset allocation across all investments. If you do not feel comfortable managing your own investments, seek the help of an investment professional.

2) When should you take distributions to pay for college costs?

In a 529 prepaid program you may not have a great deal of flexibility in the timing of your benefits because payout procedures are likely to be standardized. But this does not mean you should forget entirely about timing opportunities. The date the program makes payments to your child's school will determine the year in which the expenses are considered paid under any other tax provisions including the American Opportunity credit, the Lifetime Learning credit, and the above-the-line tuition and fees deduction. A payment of second-semester bills in January rather than December can make a significant difference in your tax liability.

With the 529 savings programs, and with most of the unit-type prepaid or guaranteed savings programs, you will have much more latitude in the timing of distributions. It is up to you to decide how to allocate your account between academic years, and when to request distributions. It appears under the current tax rules that you must carefully coordinate any cash withdrawals from your 529 savings account to fall within the same calendar year as your payment of qualifying expenses. To determine the tax consequences of your withdrawals, you will need to compare the beneficiary's total qualified expenses to total 529 withdrawals. If you pay for college costs this year, but receive your 529 plan distribution next year, you may find that you have a tax problem. The IRS may eventually develop new rules that permit some crossover in matching expenses with cash withdrawals, but any such rules would add to your recordkeeping burdens.

Keep in mind that the coordination of various tax incentives for higher education can make for very complex planning. As an example, consider that Section 529 qualified higher education expenses are reduced by expenses used to determine the American Opportunity or Lifetime Learning credit. Since the American Opportunity credit is calculated on up to $4,000 in qualified expenses, but a Lifetime Learning credit is calculated on as much as $10,000 in qualified expenses, you may find that it is better to target the 529 withdrawals to the American Opportunity credit years rather than to the Lifetime Learning credit years. The effect on the dependency support test of taking distributions from a 529 and using them for a child's education expenses is another item to be planned for. See chapter 7 for a more extensive discussion of these considerations.

3) When should you take a nonqualified distribution?

Consider taking a nonqualified distribution whenever the tax and financial aid consequences will turn out better for you than the use of your account for qualified higher education expenses. Because you will be subject to income tax and a 10 percent penalty, this tactic is not often recommended, but here are some possible scenarios where a nonqualified distribution may be beneficial:

♦ In many prepaid programs, the value of the contract for beneficiaries attending college out-of-state is limited to actual tuition at the institution being attended. A beneficiary who is enrolled in the prepaid program but later relocates to another state may find that public university tuition in the new state is lower than tuition in the old state. In this situation, canceling the contract might be better than using it to pay tuition at the lower rate.

♦ A refund of the account might make sense when its use for qualified expenses would severely impact a grant award from the school (this would not be the case with federal financial-aid awards, as discussed in chapter 4). You will not necessarily know this until your child is close to college age and you assess the prospects for financial aid. Before applying for admission, you should ask your child's targeted colleges about their policies concerning families with 529 accounts.

If a nonqualified distribution produces an unwanted result, and you have no immediate need for the funds, consider simply leaving the account alone. Unless the state imposes a time restriction, an account in a 529 savings program will continue to grow tax-deferred until you decide to take distributions, and that can be many years down the road.

4) Who should be the recipient of the distribution?

Typically, you will want the 529 plan administrator to make the distribution payable to the designated beneficiary or to the school. This way, the Form 1099-Q will be issued to the beneficiary, with nothing reported on Form 1040 provided the beneficiary incurs sufficient qualified higher education expenses. By directing the payment directly to the school, you also eliminate the risk of mismatching the year of the withdrawal and the year of the qualified expenses, but you may be creating a risk that the school will adjust your child's financial aid when it receives a check from the 529 plan. (So find out from the school first!)

As discussed in chapter 3, a distribution to you, the account owner, should also qualify as tax-free to the extent the designated beneficiary on your account incurs sufficient qualified higher education expenses. However, the Form 1099-Q will be issued to you and a checkbox on the form will indicate that you were not the beneficiary, raising a potential red flag with the IRS that could complicate your life.

If any portion of the distribution is taxable because the designated beneficiary has not incurred sufficient qualified higher education expenses, your decision as to who receives the distribution becomes even more critical, because it will determine who receives the Form 1099-Q and is responsible for reporting and paying tax on the income.

It is also possible that your choice of distributee will make a difference in determining whether you may claim your child as your dependent. See chapter 7 for further explanation.

5) Should funds be withdrawn if the beneficiary receives a scholarship?

Qualified higher education expenses (QHEE) must be adjusted to exclude tuition paid for with a tax-free grant or scholarship. If you withdraw more than the adjusted amount QHEE, the excess constitutes a nonqualified distribution. Although the earnings portion of a nonqualified distribution is taxable, a distribution made on account of a tax-free scholarship, to the extent of the scholarship, is not subject to the 10 percent penalty (see IRS Form 5329). The IRS has not indicated whether the distribution must occur in the same year as the receipt of the scholarship in order to be eligible for the penalty waiver—some tax experts feel it is permissible to look for scholarships received in prior years whenever a nonqualified distribution is taken.

If the beneficiary is in a low tax bracket, directing a scholarship distribution to that beneficiary may be much less costly than ending up with too much money in your 529 plan and ultimately taking a nonqualified distribution that is subject to the 10 percent penalty. Check to see if the beneficiary will be subject to the kiddie tax (see chapter 11) before making this decision, as the earnings may end up being taxed at a higher tax bracket.

A similar decision must be made when you or your child can claim the American Opportunity or Lifetime Learning credit. As discussed in chapter 3, qualified higher education expenses for Section 529 purposes must be adjusted to exclude the tuition used to claim the credit. As with the scholarship exception, the taxable earnings that arise from this adjustment are not subject to the 10 percent penalty. In some situations, directing the nonqualified distribution to the beneficiary can work out nicely. The parents' income may be too high to claim the American Opportunity or Lifetime Learning credit, but they can push the credit onto their child's tax return (provided they forego the dependency exemption) where the credit may be sufficient to wipe out any income tax resulting from the nonqualified distribution.

Managing Multiple Accounts

Here are several reasons to think about opening multiple accounts for the same beneficiary:

1) *To gain state tax deductions.* If you live in Virginia, for example, multiple accounts for the same beneficiary may lead to a larger tax deduction than just one account. If you live in any other state that offers a deduction for contributions, but places an annual cap on the amount of deduction, be sure to study the tax rules to determine if you are maximizing the benefit.

2) *To diversify your investments.* While some savings programs give you ample opportunity to diversify your investments within one account by spreading your contribution among different investment options, others require that you establish multiple accounts to use more than one of the available investment options. Further diversification can be achieved by establishing accounts in different 529 plans.

3) *To combine a prepaid program with a savings program.* Because prepaid programs typically cover tuition and fees only, it is becoming more common among those using prepaid programs to open a separate account with a savings program to pay for books, equipment, supplies, and room and board.

4) *To contribute an amount higher than the state's maximum contribution limit.* If the 529 plan you've chosen has a contribution cap of $300,000

and you intend to invest $350,000, you would have to open accounts in multiple states. However, you should not attempt to use multiple states as a way to deposit more than you can reasonably justify as necessary for your beneficiary's higher education expenses.

5) *To take advantage of a limited benefit.* Some states provide a tax deduction, or a partial match, for your contribution, subject to a dollar limit. While the incentive may persuade you to direct your first dollars into that program, you may decide to use a different 529 plan for contributions beyond the amount that secures the maximum benefit.

6) *To start the clock running.* Even if a particular 529 plan is not your first choice, you may want to open a small account in it if there are any benefits that require a minimum period of participation. For example, a 529 plan may require that your account be open for a minimum period of time before taking qualified distributions (this is not common). Or perhaps your state offers a program that allows your beneficiary to "vest" as a state resident for tuition if you have been in the 529 plans for a certain number of years. This can be a valuable benefit if your family moves out of state and sends a child back to a public university in that state.

7) *To reduce income taxes.* See chapter 7 for a discussion of how multiple accounts can be used to your advantage by permitting selective withdrawals based on each account's "earnings ratio."

Multiple accounts can mean multiple account maintenance fees, however, and in some programs will cause you to miss out on the fee waiver given to large accounts. Multiple accounts will also result in more statements and other collateral material coming your way from the programs.

Account Management Beyond the Basics

Advanced account management involves making changes to your account after you have established it. There are three basic categories of change, any one of which should be considered in the appropriate circumstances:

1) *Changing the designated beneficiary.* A beneficiary change can be made in most 529 plans simply by filling out a change form and submitting

it to the plan administrator. Sometimes a fee will be charged. To avoid termination of the original account, and the triggering of income tax and penalty, the new beneficiary must qualify under the Section 529 definition of "member of the family" (see chapter 3). As an alternative to a complete change of beneficiary, the owner may be able to accomplish a partial change by establishing a separate account for the new beneficiary and transferring some funds from the first account to the second through a rollover.

2) *Changing the account owner.* Most 529 plans allow the original account owner to transfer ownership of an account to another person. These programs generally do not require that the new account owner be a member of the family or have any other specific relationship to the original owner. However, some programs do not accept a request to change account owner prior to the original owner's death or incapacity, while still others spell out procedures in limited circumstances, such as when the account owner and spouse are separated or divorced. For the most part, a change in account ownership is a tax-neutral event. However, this is an area that invites IRS scrutiny and can create tax uncertainties, especially when questions surrounding the generation-skipping transfer tax arise, or where a non-individual account owner such as a corporation, trust, or other entity is involved.

3) *Transferring balances between 529 plans.* Section 529 allows a tax-free rollover from one state's 529 plan to another state's at any time as long as the beneficiary of the receiving account is a different member of the beneficiary's family. In addition, a same-beneficiary rollover can be transacted once in any 12-month period. If your 529 account has lost value, and you wish to recognize the loss for tax purposes, you should avoid making contributions to another 529 plan for the same beneficiary or for any other member of the beneficiary's family for at least 61 days following the liquidation of the loss account, so as to avoid rollover treatment.

The following strategies demonstrate the flexibility of 529 plans.

Strategy #1: When you are uncertain about college

Let's say you are attracted to the tax advantages and investment approach of a 529 plan, but have no specific plans to use your savings for your own or someone else's education. You, your children, your grandchildren, or some other family member might need education funds in the future, but you do not want to irrevocably commit your savings to that purpose. Consider establishing an account and naming yourself as beneficiary. If you later decide to fund a relative's college or graduate-school education, you can then change the beneficiary designation.

> *Example:* Joyce is a 50-year old grandmother with $30,000 invested in bank certificates of deposit. She is already funding her 401(k) account and Roth IRA to the maximum extent allowable, and has substantial assets in those retirement plans. Joyce decides to open an account in a 529 savings plan using the $30,000 received when her CDs mature so that she can now take advantage of tax deferral. She names herself as beneficiary of the account, with the idea of taking post-graduate classes in the future, although having no specific plans to do so. Ten years later, Joyce abandons the idea of returning to school and decides to change her 529 account beneficiary designation from herself to her grandson, who is now 11 years old. She makes the five-year averaging election so that the value of the gift (now $75,000) is covered by her gift tax annual exclusions. The account will continue to grow tax-deferred until Joyce withdraws the funds for her grandson's college expenses.
>
> Alternatively, Joyce can name her grandson as initial beneficiary of the account even if she thinks she may want to use the funds for her own education in the future. The advantage of this approach is that the value of the account is removed from her taxable estate now, along with future earnings and appreciation. Joyce never gives up ownership and retains the right to use the account for non-educational purposes, subject to income tax and 10 percent penalty on the accumulated earnings.
>
> With her substantial assets and a desire to shelter as much as she can from income tax and estate taxes, Joyce may decide to establish two sizable accounts: one for herself and another for her grandson. She can, for example, contribute $75,000 in 2018 to a 529 plan for her grandson and make the special five-year

election for gift tax purposes. Instead of waiting until 2023 to make an additional gift-tax-free contribution to that account, she establishes a second account with herself as beneficiary. Joyce's contributions to this account can now grow tax deferred and in 2023 she can simply change the beneficiary to her grandson and remove another $75,000—or more, if inflation adjustments cause the gift tax annual exclusion to be increased—from her estate without using any of her $11.18 million (plus inflation adjustments) lifetime exemption.

The 529 plan administrators can refuse to accept Joyce's contributions or they can terminate the account if they determine that Joyce does not intend to use the 529 account to pay the higher education expenses of the designated beneficiary.

Strategy #2: For the family that may qualify for financial aid

Chapter 4 describes how an interest in a 529 plan may impact the student's eligibility for financial aid. Let's assume you own three accounts in a 529 plan, one for each of your three children. When your oldest child enrolls in college and files the FAFSA application, all three accounts would be reportable on the FAFSA as parent assets, assessed at a maximum 5.64% rate in determining the expected family contribution (EFC). So before the FAFSA is filed, you change the registration of the 529 accounts for your two younger children to a UTMA custodian. These accounts are now considered the siblings' assets and excluded from the older child's FAFSA. CAUTION: Do not request an owner change to a grandparent or other third party in an effort to remove assets from the FAFSA unless you are fully aware of the potential negative consequences. You no longer have any rights to the 529 account, and you expose the assets to a number of risks and uncertainties, e.g. the new owner dying, being sued, or being required to spend down the account to receive Medicaid benefits. In addition, a college financial aid administrator who feels the change in ownership was improper may use "professional judgment" to include the value of the accounts as a parent asset when determining the student's expected family contribution.

If you have more to invest than your state allows as an income tax deduction, and you do not want to delay any contributions to a future year, you should consider contributing the excess amount to another state's 529 plan. In the following year, roll over to your home-state program to claim another state tax deductions. Note, however, that this particular strategy won't work if your state is one of several that restrict the deduction to non-rollover or "virgin" contributions.

If an out-of-state 529 plan is more attractive than your home state 529 plan, but your state offers a deduction for in-state contributions, you may want to direct your contributions to the in-state 529 plan and later roll over to the out-of-state 529 plan. This strategy won't work in states that require "recapture" of your deduction on outbound rollovers.

Planning for state income tax savings can be an uncertain exercise, particularly where 529 plans are concerned. Obtain the advice of a tax professional in your state.

Avoid Abusive Change Strategies in Estate Tax Planning

The rules surrounding 529 plans offer unique opportunities to reduce or eliminate estate tax, gift tax, and generation-skipping transfer tax. They also give rise to strategies that some individuals believe will allow for a large tax-free intergenerational transfer of wealth that cannot be accomplished through traditional gifting techniques. These strategies pose a challenge to the IRS as it attempts to regulate the use of Section 529, and they pose a risk to taxpayers who use them without adequately considering the consequences of an IRS challenge. For example, consider the following "loophole":

> *Example:* John wants to contribute $300,000 to a 529 plan for his son Freddy while avoiding gift taxes. He can contribute only $75,000 this year under the special five-year election without creating a taxable gift. However, John also has three nieces, so he

decides to establish and fund with $75,000 a 529 account for each niece. The five-year election shelters these contributions from gift tax. John figures that he can change the beneficiary designation on those three accounts to his son whenever he wants without further consequences. Because the cousins are the same generation as his son, the changes in beneficiary are not gifts (see chapter 9).

This maneuver is an end run around the gift tax annual exclusion limits, and the IRS will probably not be happy with it. But how can this apparent abuse be distinguished from a situation where John truly intends to help fund the future college expenses of his nieces, and only because of unforeseeable circumstances does he find it necessary to later change the beneficiary to his own son?

There are similar "opportunities" to leverage the annual exclusion through other family members. For instance, John conceivably could have established 529 accounts for his own five brothers and their wives using the available annual exclusions to place hundreds of thousands of dollars into tax-deferred investment accounts, removing these assets from his estate without incurring gift tax. The substitution of his son as designated beneficiary on these accounts would be deemed a gift from these extended family members to John's son due to the difference in generations, but the gift tax annual exclusions of each of those relatives can be used to avoid gift tax consequences.

To carry this to its absurd conclusion, consider how you might try to create a tax problem for your least favorite relative.

Example: Ed never forgave his brother Sean for taking, and then losing, his baseball card collection 40 years ago and now sees an opportunity to make him pay for it. In 2018, Ed contributes $75,000 to a 529 plan, designating Sean as the account beneficiary and electing five-year treatment to avoid any gift tax consequences. As owner of the account, Ed immediately changes the beneficiary from Sean to Ed's son, Kyle. Sean is never aware of his brother's actions, which according to the IRS' proposed regulations create a gift from Sean to his nephew Kyle (Kyle belongs to a lower generation than Sean). Sean understandably fails to make the five-year election, and so has unwittingly made a taxable gift that utilizes part of his $11.18 million lifetime exemption. Ed lets Sean know about his maneuvers after it is too late to do anything about it, and Sean realizes that he has now lost some of his lifetime exemption, or even worse, has failed to report a taxable gift and now is subject to gift taxes, interest, and possible penalties.

Although donative intent is not required for the federal gift tax to apply, it seems unfair that an unsuspecting donor would end up stuck with a gift tax liability. Perhaps the final regulations under Section 529 should require that the original intended beneficiary "accept" the designation before the gift of a 529 contribution can be considered completed. Rules similar to the qualified disclaimer provisions of the Internal Revenue Code could accomplish this. In the above example, Sean would have had the opportunity to smell the trap and refuse the position of designated beneficiary.

The ability to change account owner can also lead to abuse. The mere act of transferring ownership appears to have no federal income tax or gift tax consequences. This follows the tax logic underlying Section 529, provided the 529 account is ultimately expended for the beneficiary's qualified higher education expenses. But what happens if the new account owner requests a refund of the account balance? Is there a gift tax consequence? If the answer is no, then the opportunity presents itself to transfer wealth without making a gift.

Example: Shirley is a wealthy grandmother making maximum annual exclusion gifts to her son Todd and her grandson Timmy. Todd is wealthy in his own right and making his own annual exclusion gifts to Timmy. To bypass Todd's generation and funnel more of the family wealth to her grandson, Shirley establishes a 529 account for Todd, using the money she normally gifts directly to him. Shirley then transfers ownership of the 529 account to Timmy so Timmy becomes the account owner with his father as the beneficiary. Timmy simply requests a refund from the 529 plan and receives the money without any gift tax (although generation-skipping transfer tax may still be a concern).

Example: Charlie is another wealthy individual who plays cards in Shirley's bridge club. When Charlie hears what Shirley has done with her 529 account, he decides he can go even further in transferring millions of dollars to his children simply by opening dozens of 529 accounts and naming a different friend or neighbor as designated beneficiary to each account. He fully funds each account with $75,000 under the five-year election, avoiding gift taxes. He changes the ownership of the accounts to his children, who then request refunds of the millions in assets without further transfer tax consequences.

An often-heard phrase is "if it's too good to be true, it probably is." Section 529 of the Internal Revenue Code challenges that notion, especially in the area of estate and gift taxes. There is no question that the law provides unique and unconventional benefits, but Congress has signaled its concern about the potential for tax abuse with 529 plans, and the IRS is sure to challenge any transactions similar to Shirley's and Charlie's. The best advice is to stay within reasonable bounds and remember that 529 plans are intended to be a tax-advantaged college savings vehicle, not a tax shelter.

THIRTEEN

The Role of a Financial Advisor

Prior to 2001, when the first broker-sold 529 plans were introduced, financial advisors typically recommended traditional investment products such as Roth IRAs or mutual funds to their clients saving for college. Since then, the landscape has changed dramatically and advisors now recognize that 529 plans can be a key tool to help clients reach their goals. Today, there are 30 advisor-sold plans that offer a wide range of commission-based investment options. Yet brokers aren't the only ones recommending 529 plans. In recent years, the financial services industry has seen a movement toward fee-based Registered Investment Advisers (RIAs), who assist families with selecting and managing no-load 529 plan options.

Advisors, whether working for a broker-dealer or RIA, need to recognize the growing impact these once modest accounts can have on their business. In 2002, the average account balance across all 529 plans was just over $9,500. By Q4 2017, that figure had risen to over $24,000, a 150% increase[1]. With college costs rising twice as fast as any other household expense, 529 average account balances should continue to grow.

---

1. College Savings Plans Network. "September 2014 529 Report."

Families can likely expect to pay much more than the average household income if they want to send their newborn child to a four-year private college in 18 years. Although scholarships and grants will still exist to help cover some of the cost, this is becoming an ever-alarming expenditure. In fact, college costs are the number one household concern among parents[2]. So much so that 52% of parents say saving for their children's education is more important than saving for their own retirement[3]. More than ever before, parents and grandparents are seeking out financial professionals to assist them in planning for college, and advisors need to be prepared. This chapter will examine how you can incorporate 529 plans into discussions with your clients, and how to leverage these vehicles to create opportunities to grow your practice.

How do I begin the initial discussion?

You don't have to limit your 529 plan discussions to families with young children. While this group is obviously the most suitable, you may also have clients saving for college for nieces, nephews, grandchildren or even themselves. There is no one type of client that is the perfect fit for a 529 plan because anyone can open an account and name almost anyone as the beneficiary.

Once you've determined that your client can use help with educational planning, the next step is to discuss which savings vehicle is their best option. This book has listed the merits and downfalls of different college savings vehicles, so for this chapter we'll discuss how to proceed if you and your client determine that a 529 plan is the recommended choice.

Should I always recommend an in-state 529 plan?

Currently, 34 states and the District of Columbia offer residents a tax deduction or credit for 529 plan contributions. However, all but seven

---

2. Gallup. "2001-2015 Economy and Personal Finance Survey"
3. T. Rowe Price. "Parents, Kids & Money Survey." 2014.

of these states require clients to invest in their home state's plan in order to receive the tax break. Some states will also disregard the account balance of students with in-state 529 plans when determining eligibility for state-funded financial aid. As an advisor, it is your obligation to make your client aware of these benefits. In fact, the Municipal Securities Rulemaking Board requires anyone giving financial advice regarding 529 plans to notify clients if investing in another state's plan will cause them to lose out on these perks.

That is not to say that investing in an out-of-state plan is never prudent. Obviously if your client resides in a state that does not afford a tax benefit or lives in a state with no income tax, you should be looking at all plans available. Sometimes an out-of-state plan may be the best option even when the in-state plan does offer special tax benefits. The key is to properly weigh the pros and cons for your client to ensure they are maximizing their savings potential.

How do I compare plans?

529 plans are complex investment vehicles and contain certain attributes that won't be found elsewhere in the investing space. There are over 100 different plans, so the question becomes: How do I compare them all? Savingforcollege.com offers a convenient 529 plan comparison tool with detailed information on every plan in one place.

The comparison tool allows you to build a customized list of plans based on criteria that you select. If you're working with a client who has a couple of plans in mind, you can view a list of all plans by state, click on your choices, and generate a side-by-side comparison. If you don't know the names of the plans you want to research, you can create a list of plans

To use the plan comparison tool, please visit Savingforcollege.com/compare

based on features that your client is looking for. The tool also allows you to filter your results by direct-sold, broker-sold or prepaid plans.

Attributes such as investment management, fees and expenses, contribution limits and resident benefits all need to be considered when making a recommendation to a client. Sure, a state may afford your client a tax deduction, but if the plan's fees are 50 basis points higher than another, how much is that deduction actually worth? The in-state plan could also have limited investment options or lagging performance compared to its competitors. So let's look at a detailed example to see how all of these features might come into play.

> *Example:* You are a registered representative working for a broker-dealer firm. You and your client, Bob, have decided that a 529 plan is the best way to save for his 3-year old child's college education. Bob has great expectations for his son and wants to save for a 4-year private school as well as a graduate degree. Bob currently lives in Georgia, which offers residents a tax deduction up to $2,000 ($4,000 if married filing jointly) if they invest in an in-state plan. However, the plan does not have many investment options and it also has a very low maximum lifetime contribution amount (currently $235,000). Given the future cost of college, you determine that Bob conservatively needs to save around $500 a month in order to save for dual degrees.
>
> During the discussion, you make the following recommendations after getting approval from your firm: Bob should put $167 a month into the Georgia Path2college 529 plan. The plan's fees are actually quite low and this contribution schedule will still allow him to take maximum advantage of the $2,000 state tax deduction each year. However, you explain to him that the plan has a limited menu of investment options as well as a low contribution ceiling. Even if Bob were to contribute the maximum amount allowed, he might not be able to save enough for two degrees.
>
> You suggest that Bob put the other $333 a month into a broker-sold, out-of-state plan that offers a bevy of investment options. It allows you as an advisor to place him into investments you feel can

beat the rising cost of education. You will also be able to monitor the account just as you do with Bob's other investments.

The example above is a good way to provide added value to a client. You've helped him maximize his state tax deduction and demonstrated your knowledge of the markets by recommending the out-of-state plan. Remember, 529 plans are one of the few investments which clients can open themselves (usually at no cost), so be wise with your investment choices if you suggest a broker-sold plan.

Special Cases

Millennial Clients

Nearly 20% of parents who are looking to open a 529 plan are between 25 and 34 years old[4]. There is a projected $30 trillion transfer of wealth coming from Baby Boomers to this younger generation coming, so it is critical for financial advisors to begin to attract millennial clients. However, millennials do not operate like previous generations. They are skeptics of the financial services industry in the aftermath of the 2008 financial crisis and having seen their parents lose vast sums of their wealth. .

Studies have shown that this skepticism has caused millennials to shy away from many financial products traditionally offered through advisors. However, they do seem to have a keen interest in saving for their children's college education. Many of them are feeling the burden of student debt and are committed to saving in order to reduce their children's dependency on loans.

Helping young families understand and invest in 529 plans can be critical to forming new relationships and securing future business, but you must be careful with your approach. According to a Pew Research paper from 2014, as a generation, millennials are about half as likely to trust people as Baby Boomers. They believe in themselves and with unlimited

4. Savingforcollege.com. "Annual Survey." 2015.

access to information, they are confident that they can handle their own investments. Here are a few key points on how to handle millennials in the college savings space.

1) *Be straightforward.* Over 23% of millennials have earned a bachelor's degree or higher, making them the most educated generation in history[5]. You can expect everything in your conversations to be researched and scrutinized, so always be direct and truthful when discussing any financial product or plan. When discussing 529 plans, simply list out the pros and the cons. Overhyping them as an investment will only hurt your credibility.

2) *Provide options.* Millennials are independent thinkers who do not appreciate being told what to do. When presenting a college savings strategy, be sure to provide multiple options that include different plans, contribution amounts and investments and outline the pros and cons of each. Allow the client to review the different scenarios and involve them in the decision making process.

3) *Educate.* Millennial clients will also want to know *why* each plan option is being presented. Remember, they will do their own research so if they don't understand why you've selected certain 529 plans it can lead to confusion. What's more, discussing the reasoning behind your selections might reveal valuable information about your client's investment preferences. For example, when you explain why you chose a foreign equity fund for their 529 portfolio, you may find out that they are more interested in socially responsible investments. Having this discussion will allow you to create specially catered advice, which is of utter importance to a generation that demands mass customization.

Demonstrating your expertise and gaining the trust of this skeptical generation will give you access into other areas of their financial lives, which they currently may be handling on their own. For example, becoming a parent is a life-altering event, which opens the door to cross-sell products such as life insurance. Not only is the millennial generation

---

5. Hyder, Shama. *Here's What You Need To Know About Millennials.*Forbes, 4 Mar. 2014.

incredibly underinsured, they are twice as likely to buy insurance online instead of through an agent[6]. In fact, a study was conducted by public relations agency Edelman gauging how the public views the trustworthiness of major industrial sectors. What topped the list? Technology. Dead last? Financial Services. As we see more and more clients purchasing financial services products online, an opportunity exists for advisors to prove their trustworthiness and reclaim the business.

Grandparents

72% of grandparents feel it's important to save for their grandchildren's higher education[7]. Those already saving plan to give a median of $25,000 to all of their grandchildren and 35% are planning to give $50,000 or more[8]. This demographic can be a lucrative one for any advisor providing college planning services. 529 plans are a great investment for grandparents, but there are some important things to consider.

On the surface, grandparent-owned 529 plans work just the same as any other one. They can use any state's 529 plan, enjoy tax-free gains when the funds are used for qualified higher education expenses, and may be eligible for state tax deductions on their contributions. Ownership of the funds also remains with the grandparent, which means all distributions will be made at their discretion. It's when we dig a little deeper we see some additional advantages as well as some hidden disadvantages.

Most advisors should already be offering estate planning advice to older clients, so 529 plans are a perfect way to kill two birds with one stone. Contributions to a 529 plan are treated as gifts to the beneficiary for tax and generation-skipping transfer tax purposes, and deposits up to $15,000 ($30,000 for a couple) per grandchild per year will qualify for the annual gift tax exclusion. Accounts can also be "Superfunded" by contributing 5 years worth of gifts at once (per grandchild).

---

6. Gallup. *"Insurance Companies Have a Big Problem with Millennials"* 5 Mar. 2015.

7. Hellmich, Nancy. *Most grandparents want to help fund grandkids' college.* USA Today, 21 Aug. 2014.

8. *Id.*

Example: Mr. and Mrs. Smith have eight grandchildren. They express an interest in saving for their college educations. You advise them that 529 plans are a great, tax-advantaged way to save for college: they can be the account owner; they can easily name successor owners; and funds remain in their name. They are thrilled with your advice, but become overjoyed when you inform them that by opening up a 529 account for each of their grand-children, they can remove $1.2 million from their estate in 1 day ($150,000 contributed to eight 529 plans).

A topic that warrants a discussion with any grandparent thinking of investing in a 529 plan is the potential effect on Medicaid. Elderly clients might rely heavily on this government benefit, so it is your duty as an advisor to explain the possible pitfalls. Account owners retain control of funds within a 529 plan even after the beneficiary turns 18. This retained ownership means that money in a 529 is a countable asset for Medicaid purposes. If something were to happen and your client needed nursing home care, all money within a the plan would need to be exhausted before Medicaid would pay the nursing home bills. Exhausting this account means not only liquidating a dedicated college fund, but also subjecting your gains to taxes and a 10% penalty. However, there is a possible solution to this problem.

Example: You can suggest your client transfer ownership of the account to the child's parents, but you must inform them that this is considered a transfer of assets, which will trigger a Medicaid penalty period. This period is determined by how much you trans-fer and what Medicaid determines the average private pay cost for a nursing home to be in your state. So, if your client transfers a 529 plan with $50,000 in it, and Medicaid determines the average monthly cost of a nursing home in his state is $5,000, he will be ineligible for 10 months ($50,000/$5,000).

One of the most crucial topics you'll want to discuss with grand-parents is the impact on the student's financial aid eligibility. The funds in a grandparent-owned 529 plan are not reported as assets on the Free Application for Federal Student Aid (FAFSA). However, withdrawals used for the beneficiary's qualified higher education expenses will be treated as the student's unearned income. This will have to be recorded on the grandchild's FAFSA application the following year and can reduce their aid package by up to 50% of the distribution amount.

Fortunately, there are ways to plan around this.

1) If the family is not planning on applying for financial aid, or is phased out due to their income, this is not a problem.

2) Change ownership of the plan to the parent after the child applies for financial aid. Be sure your client's plan allows for a change of ownership, as not all do. If the plan does not, you can roll over the assets to a plan that does and transfer ownership at that time. Just be careful if the client has been claiming state tax deductions for contributions to a current plan. Some states may require recapture tax on out of state rollovers or ownership changes. Additionally, remember to balance this with the potential Medicaid penalty discussed above.

3) Wait until after January 1 of the child's sophomore year in college, if the child expects to graduate in 4 years. Since the base year of the FAFSA is the prior-prior year, any income earned by the child on or after that date will not be reported on a subsequent year's FAFSA. If the child will need 5 years to graduate, wait until January 1 of the junior year in college.

College Planning

As tuition costs and the need for a college degree increase, so will your clients' expectations. Helping families save for college requires much more than simply recommending an investment vehicle like a 529 plan and telling them how much to contribute. There are many ways you can provide assistance, beginning with the application process. In fact, a study released by Fidelity stated that over a quarter of parents saving for college expect their advisor to help their child decide on a major[9]. This is an opportunity

9. Fidelity Investments. "College Savings Indicator Study." 2014.

for you to present yourself as an objective third party who can provide valuable insight and go beyond the normal expectations of an advisor.

Scholarship and Grant Search

With students graduating with an average debt load of $30,000, finding scholarships and grants to bring costs down has become more important than ever. Just because a student isn't a star athlete or academic genius doesn't mean they can't get a scholarship to college. Talk with your client about other possibilities – are they involved in any extracurricular activities? Does your company offer scholarships? Is the family part of a minority ethnic group? These are all common ways to find tuition money.

And don't worry if you're dealing with an upper-income family. According to Sallie Mae's 2014 How America Pays for College report, high-income families paid around 20 percent of their college expenses with scholarship money. What's more, 38 percent of scholarships were awarded to families with annual incomes over $100,000.

School Selection Dialogue

When helping a family choose the proper higher education institution, you need to consider both the family's financial situation and the child's needs. Clients whose children are getting a full ride to their top choice are not the norm, and would likely not need advice on college financing. But for those who do need to cover some of the costs, it's your job to present a set of options that both fit their budget and provide their child with an appropriate environment to foster success.

If your client's children are young, you won't need to focus on a specific school. Instead, simply ask whether they would like to save for a four-year private or public institution and help calculate the future cost of tuition. However, as the student gets closer to college, school selection becomes of critical importance. A dialogue about how they would like to approach paying for tuition, room & board, etc. is vital. Of course, some clients will be willing to pay whatever is required out-of-pocket. But other parents (although they may have the financial means) will want their kids to have 'some skin in the game' and are comfortable with some student loans. And you'll also likely encounter families who do not have the means to pay for full tuition, and do not want their child taking out excess loans. These clients will need help narrowing down their search to more affordable schools.

This dialogue should also involve the future college attendee, as he or she should have some input in the decision. There is no single school that is perfect for everyone. You'll want to get a better idea of things like whether the student would feel more comfortable at a small or large school, or if they want to attend a school with a historically good basketball or football team. Academic-driven students, for instance, might want to narrow their search to schools that foster the best environment for their future major. And of course, admission requirements such as SAT/ACT scores, GPA and class rank also need to be factored into this search.

Once you have a better overall picture of your client's situation and the type of school they are interested in, you can begin researching the costs. If the family already has specific colleges in mind, you can start by finding out the true price of attendance of each. Some advisors may have their own proprietary technology for this research, but those who don't can reference the college's net price calculator.

The Higher Education Act of 1965 (HEA) was amended in 2011 to require each postsecondary institution that participates in Title IV federal student aid programs to include a net price calculator on their web site. These calculators use institutional data to provide estimated net price information to current and prospective students based on the each child's situation as well as the school's availability of funds. Advisors can input the family's financial information and receive the true cost of attendance at each school. You may find that the school with the highest sticker price may be cheapest to attend after all grants and scholarships are accounted for.

When presenting the costs of different schools to a client, you may also want to include a breakdown of how much the student's loan payments would be after graduation. This can help them to weigh the pros and cons of each choice. For example, their top choice school might cost another $250 a month in loans after graduation compared to their second choice school.

Financial Aid

AGI Tactics

Another extremely valuable service you can provide to your clients is to increase their financial aid eligibility. One way to achieve this is to keep a handful of tactics up your sleeve that can lower their adjusted gross income (AGI). Colleges calculate how much a family can afford to spend on higher education before they award an aid package. When a family's AGI is reduced, their Expected Family Contribution (EFC) will also go down. Simply put, the lower a family's EFC, the more aid they will be eligible for.

Real Estate. Becoming a landlord can be a great way to bring in monthly income, while adding $0 to your AGI. This is because real estate, in most cases, allows for a depreciation deduction. If your client were to bring in net rental income equal to the depreciation deduction you get (e.g., $8,000 in income after expenses and a $8,000 deduction), there will be no effect on the family's AGI.

Capital Gains & Losses. Selling stocks and bonds may have an effect on a family's AGI if the sale triggers a capital gain or loss. For instance, you'll want to keep a close eye on transactions that occur from January of the student's junior year of high school until their junior year of college (when the family would be applying for financial aid). If the client sells a stock or bond that results in a capital gain, it will be reported as base-year income on the FAFSA. However, some strategically timed losses can help. If the sale triggers a capital loss, it would reduce AGI and could increase financial aid eligibility.

> *Example.* Bob has money invested in the stock market. Some of his positions are up, and some are down. With his child attending college soon, you advise him to just sell off the down positions triggering a $10,000 capital loss. Not only will he pay less in taxes this year, you'll reduce his AGI on the FAFSA by $3,000 each year for the next three years and by $1,000 in his child's senior year (capital losses can be carried forward). This could lead to thousands of

dollars more in federal aid for his child, taking some of the pain away from that $10,000 loss.

Social Security. If you have clients who are age 62 or older and have a child applying for financial aid you should encourage them to delay taking social security. Although they will currently forego monthly income, it will lower their AGI and increase the student's aid eligibility.

IRA Conversion. There are times when converting a pretax IRA to a Roth IRA makes sense for your client, but if they have a child applying for need-based aid; you might want to encourage them to wait. Converting to a Roth will trigger income that needs to be reported and lower their potential aid package.

Utilizing the FAFSA

One of the most difficult aspects of a financial advisor's job is getting a complete picture of a client's finances. Many times clients will 'hide' or fail to mention certain blocks of their wealth for a number of reasons. If you have a client whose child is going to be attending college soon and they plan on applying for financial aid, you have one of the best tools for detecting these concealed assets; the FAFSA.

Helping a family complete the FAFSA is an important part of the college planning process. As mentioned in Chapter 4, as an advisor, you can provide valuable insights on how to leverage certain tactics that can lead to a more lucrative award. But in order to do so, your clients will have to provide documents such as their most recent federal income tax returns, W-2s and other records of money earned, bank statements, records of investments, and records of untaxed income. Families who were previously hesitant to reveal this information should be much more cooperative when their financial aid eligibility depends on it.

In fact, the penalties for providing false or misleading information on the FAFSA include, but are not limited to, fines of up to $20,000, up to five years in jail, and repaying the financial aid received by the student. Some universities may suspend or expel a student for providing false information as well. The result of all this is usually a cooperative, truthful client giving you their complete financial picture, allowing you to provide better advice and cross-sell other products they may need.

FOURTEEN

529 ABLE Accounts

I n 2014, the Achieving a Better Life Experience (ABLE) Act was signed into law, creating an opportunity for individuals living with a disability to be able to save for education and other expenses without jeopardizing eligibility for public benefits.

The need for ABLE accounts

Nearly one in five people in the U.S. are living with a disability, according to data from the Center for Disease Control and Prevention. According to advocacy group Autism Speaks, the costs of raising a child with special needs can exceed $2 million over the course of a lifetime. In addition to education costs, parents are responsible for doctor visits, medical equipment, therapy and other necessary expenses. For many of their children, achieving financial independence as an adult is often an unrealistic goal.

Prior to the ABLE Act, if you were living with a disability and earned more than $700 a month or had more than $2,000 in assets you risked having to forfeit eligibility for Medicaid and Supplemental Security Income (SSI). Because of these limitations, there has been little incentive for individuals with disabilities to save money, and many live below the poverty level.

Today, 529 ABLE programs allow qualified individuals to save over $300,000 in a tax-advantaged account as a supplement to public assistance. However, once the account reaches $100,000 the individual is no longer eligible to receive SSI benefits, but they still qualify for Medicaid.

How 529 ABLE accounts work

Similar to a traditional 529 savings plan, a 529 ABLE account is an investment vehicle where earnings grow tax-free and are not taxed when distributions are used to pay for qualified disability expenses. Over 30 states have administered ABLE programs, and at least 10 more have passed legislation to enact them. Initially, individuals were required to use their home state's ABLE program, but the PATH Act of 2015 lifted the residency requirements. Consumers now have the ability to research each plan's fees, investment performance and program manager to find the best program to suit their needs. Each program offers multiple investment options with varying degrees of risk, including FDIC insured options.

In 2018, individuals can contribute up to $15,000 to an ABLE program, which is also the amount of the annual gift tax exclusion. Lifetime limits vary by plan and mirror the administering state's limits for 529 savings plans, which can be as high as $511,000. However, not all states that offer a tax benefit for contributions to a 529 savings plan offer the same benefit for ABLE plan contributions. Currently, there are only nine states offering a tax deduction for contributions to an ABLE program.

To be eligible for an ABLE account, an individual must have been diagnosed with a disability before age 26, with a condition expected to last at least 12 consecutive months and who are receiving benefits under SSI or Social Security Disability Insurance (SSDI). Those who are not receiving benefits must obtain a disability certificate from a doctor. Qualified disability expenses include costs of education, job training and support, healthcare and financial management.

Availability and distribution of ABLE accounts

According to research firm Strategic Insight, as of March 31, 2017 over 20,000 accounts have been opened.[1] Unlike traditional 529 savings plans, ABLE plans are not sold through financial advisors. Advisors can inform clients with special needs about ABLE programs, but the individual will have to enroll and manage the account on their own.

529 plan rollovers

The Tax Cuts and Jobs Act of 2017 included a change to allow tax-free rollovers of up to $15,000 from a traditional 529 savings plan to an ABLE account. This was an important change for families who had been saving in a 529 plan and later learned that the beneficiary was diagnosed with a disability such as Autism. Prior to the law, families in this situation may have been left with no other choice but to take a non-qualified distribution from the account. The 10% penalty on non-qualified withdrawals is waived if the beneficiary becomes disabled, but the earnings would be subject to income tax.

Yet while an ABLE rollover will be *federal* tax free, individuals may still be subject to state tax on the earnings portion of the rollover. Some states have not conformed to federal tax law regarding rollovers and would still consider a rollover from a 529 savings plan to a 529 ABLE program a non-qualified distribution. Individuals should consult a tax advisor as to the appropriate state tax treatment of the earnings portion of the distribution.

Drawbacks of ABLE programs

For individuals with special needs, the ABLE Act was one of the most significant pieces of legislation since the American Disabilities Act of 1990. However, ABLE accounts will most likely serve as a supplement to a Special Needs Trust, which can be funded with more than $15,000 per year

---

1. 1Q 2018 Strategic Insight 529 and ABLE Data Highlights, May 10, 2018.

and can have balances above $100,000 without affecting SSI. Financial planners specializing in Special Needs Planning can provide oversight, financial management and planning strategies for the trust, but would not be able to provide the same services with an ABLE account.

Another reason individuals may be hesitant to enroll in an ABLE account is the Medicaid payback requirement. The ABLE Act includes a provision that allows states to seek reimbursement for Medicaid payments upon the death of the account owner if there are any remaining funds in the account. The state becomes a creditor and has a lien on the ABLE account. There is no Medicaid payback required with a Special Needs Trust.

Index

26659258R00115

Made in the USA
Columbia, SC
12 September 2018